DECISIONS

THE POWER TO OVERCOME
SELF-DEFEATING BEHAVIORS

By:

Sean Douglas

Decisions

Cover photograph by Jay Perez at 2Ps Photography
www.Facebook.com/2PsPhoto

Follow Sean Douglas @ www.Facebook.com/SeanDouglasSpeaks

ISBN-10:1532943865

ISBN-13: 978-1532943867

DEDICATION

❖

This book is dedicated to my wife, Candi, who has stuck by me through all my issues, all my adversity, and we have somehow made it through it all. I am so grateful to have such a loving woman in my life. I can't thank you enough for putting up with me. I look forward to the future.

TABLE OF CONTENTS

Acknowledgements

My first thanks goes to my Lord and Savior Jesus Christ. A dream was put in my heart and I finally have the courage to make it a reality.

To my family. I can't think of one person in my family who hasn't tried to help me, boost my confidence, or point me in the right direction so that I may succeed. I love you guys and I am so thankful I have a family so supportive and loving.

To my sister Kathy. We've had a rough relationship but I value you more than you know. Thank you so much for enduring while you have read and edited this book. I couldn't have done this without you. I love you.

TJ. You're like a brother to me and we have done so many stupid things in our lives that we made each other's childhoods memorable. I couldn't ask for a better partner in crime and I wouldn't take back anything that happened. I look forward to many more memories, except this time we'll make sure they're smarter than when we were younger. I love you brother!

Grandpa G. How do I express my thankfulness to you? I know you're looking down on us from Heaven. I miss you terribly and my heart hurts that I can't pick up the phone just to chat. Thank you for being the rock in our lives and someone we looked to for guidance and wisdom. I love you so much.

To my Mother. I love you so much and you are one of the strongest women I know. From rising out of despair to building one of the most successful home health care businesses and going back to school to get your degree. I am so proud of what you have accomplished. Keep being the change people need in their lives.

Decisions

To my Father. I am so thankful for you for pushing me to succeed and being one of the biggest mentors in my life. My little league coach, military coach, marriage coach, I have relied on you much more than most people will ever realize. I love you very much and I am so grateful for our relationship.

Stan Williams. Thank you for mentoring me in the resilience world and I couldn't have asked for a better trainer, mentor, and friend. I am so grateful for everything you have done for me. Words can't express the ups and downs in my life and the impact that you have had to keep me fighting every day. I wish you the best in everything you do, and you will impact so many lives. I can't wait to see what God's plans are for your life.

Richard Lambert. Thank you so much for seeing something inside of me that you thought I would make a great Resilience Trainer. I have enjoyed working with you and I look forward to continued friendship and partnership in the resilience initiative. Thank you so much for everything you do.

Mike Phillips. I can't thank you enough for your guidance and wisdom. I can call you at any time and you know exactly what to say to calm me down, pick up me up, and get me moving again. I am so happy to have you in my life.

Stephen Scoggins and Josh Bledsoe. If it weren't for you guys I would still be sitting on my couch wondering "What if?" You both have been a huge part of me writing this book, building my speaking business and career, to discovering my purpose and to have the courage to follow my dreams. You are some of the most influential people in my life and my biggest fans. Thank You, Thank You, Thank You!

Decisions

To all my military brothers and sisters. It was a pleasure serving with you. All my Military Training Instructor brothers and sisters, I had a blast learning from each and every one of you and it was a pleasure training with you. I will never forget the friendships, relationships, and the amazing leaders I have had the pleasure of serving under, and learning from. For over a decade, the military has been my family and I love all you. Be strong, be safe, and you will always be remembered.

Introduction

I wrote this book unknowingly. I woke up one night unable to breathe, scared. It was as if someone was standing on my chest and it was very hard to catch my breath. As I sat there in the darkness, thoughts and feelings from different time periods of my life began to come and go like the ocean waves. Events that I had forgotten about, feelings about difficult situations in my life, and childhood memories dominated my every thought. I didn't know why this happening. I tried to write down as many thoughts and feelings as I could. I calmed down and went back to sleep. A week or so later, the same experience happened again. I was scared that this would be a constant event, and when it would end. After I wrote down everything that flooded my mind, I went to sleep and that was the last time it happened. A few days later, I was reading my scribbles and notes and was amazed at what I had written. I started finishing the sentences and a book was born.

This book is my first. It's an autobiographical approach to my story. A story of a kid growing up in a domestic violence and alcohol dominated household. A story of living in a step-family, my grandparents' basement, joining the military, living in a car and on friend's couches, contemplating suicide, marriage, battling addiction, and overcoming my self-defeating behaviors. I hope someone reads this, identifies with my story, and learns something in order to help and inspire someone else to change.

Through this process, I have become stronger. I was embarrassed at how I lived my life, how I grew up, and the struggles I have endured throughout the course of my

Decisions

life. I know now that my pain was all part of the process. I am able to discuss the struggles in my life and help others to succeed in their struggle as well. I want to inspire the uninspired. My goal is for someone that because they heard my testimony, because of what I have said or done, they look at me and tell me they have decided not to give up. My passion and purpose is to help as many people that I can live their dream life.

I hope you, the reader, is inspired after reading my story. I have interwoven teaching and learning points throughout the book with quotes that tie everything together. Read ahead, enjoy the book, go out and inspire the uninspired, and "Live Your Brand."

Decisions

MY STORY BEGINS

1

What's the hardest decision you've ever had to make? At some point in your life you were faced with a monumental choice; chances are, you sat down and worked out the pros of cons of this life changing decision you were about to make. Most of us have family, friends, or co-workers to communicate our ideas with to ensure we choose the best possible path. There are also times where we rush into a situation not fully considering the outcome and life quickly becomes unbearable.

Growing up in Michigan can be funny, yet exhausting. Have you ever gotten frost bite and sunburned all in the same week? Have you ever had to flip back and forth between three different news channels just to make sure they didn't miss your school on the "Snow Day - Closed" List, then the next morning you're walking to school through what felt like an Arctic Tundra, two feet of snow, uphill a few miles, one way with one glove? According to my mom, she has made this trek many times, in fact, she would tell me every time I would complain about doing my chores.

On the other hand, living in Michigan inspired me to have dreams for my future. As long as I can remember, I have wanted to be a farmer. My dad's dad - we call him "Papa D"- lives on a ten acre lot in New Haven, MI. To me, a kid living right outside the city of Detroit, this was

Decisions

considered going "up north" to the country. The house sits a small distance from the road, surrounded by a horse pasture on both sides that stretches to the wood line at the back of the 10 acre property. I could feel the anticipation building as we got off the freeway and went through this little farm town because I knew on the other side I would see horses, pheasants, and hear my grandmother's soft, southern voice. I spent a lot of time there because it was where I always felt the safest.

When I was in first grade, my mom and dad divorced after he made the decision to join the U.S. Air Force. I never fully understood why he made the decision to leave after already having a wife and three children, but I do know it was something in his heart that he was very passionate about. My mom made the decision to file divorce papers while my dad was away at training, and that started a ripple effect that I feel still affects me today.

My childhood was spent bouncing back and forth between my mom and dad's house, with every other weekend spent with our dad. I was young and didn't quite understand the process. Therefore, my older sister, who is three years older than I am, was who I relied heavily on for guidance. My other sister, three years younger than me, just kind of followed us and did as we did. I always looked forward to seeing my dad's side of the family because it seemed as if they were so carefree, and very loving. My father's brother, Tony, and I would sit for hours in the rocking chair listening to his Marty Robbins records next to the fireplace. I loved sitting on his lap listening to the pops and crackles of the fire burning as the warm glow from the embers lit the den. I listened to Marty Robbins' songs pretending that I was the gunfighter in the saloon, the rancher on a cattle trail, or the US Marshall looking for an outlaw. I knew, in those moments, that whenever I was

Decisions

visiting Uncle Tony and Aunt Carrie's house, that that's what a family was supposed to be and nothing could ever hurt me.

Aunt Carrie had a unique way of losing her hearing when you wanted something and didn't ask properly. I would always get sucked into repeating myself three or four times before realizing that I needed to say "please" and "thank you". She never gave up on instilling customs and courtesies in me, and for that I am grateful. There was no swearing, talking back, or temper tantrums raised at this house, because although soap looks harmless, it has a very bitter taste when rubbed against your teeth. My sisters and I knew the line and we knew better to stay on the right side of it or the soap was coming out.

Being back at home, however, was a different story. I can't say it was all bad, but I wouldn't want to experience it again. My mom met a guy after the divorce between her and my dad was final. Our new family of five moved to a different house, which would be the first of many. My two sisters and I slept in the same room in this large two story house. This was every kid's dream house; the kind where you can play Hide-and-Seek and not use the same hiding spot twice. The three of us had all picked out our own rooms, but we stayed in the downstairs bedroom for the few months we lived there. We had to move to another house for some reason unknown to me, and where we went next was where I would meet my best friend.

A couple houses down from ours lived this young boy my age who was always driving a red Power Wheels jeep. The other kids on the street always wanted a turn, but he never let anyone drive it. I spent that summer preparing for second grade at a new school, as well as getting to know the guy who would eventually become

Decisions

what I didn't want as a father figure and my mom's husband. I would be introduced to wooden paddles, belts, and many visits to the corner for my "misbehavior". There was something awful about mine and my sister's names written onto the thick end of a piece of wood used to spank us. It frightened me to the point of spending as much time as I could playing with my new friend to stay out of the house. We became as close as brothers while spending long afternoons building Lego cities, having sleepovers at his house, and playing "Army" every chance we got. I found out after spending a few days at his house that he was in fact paralyzed from the waist down, which was why he was always in his jeep outside. Inside, he crawled around on his hands, dragging his legs behind him like a seal, and was the most honest, loving, understanding person I had ever met. His mom welcomed me as part of the family and it was so hard to leave them, as yet again, we had to move about a year later when my mom married the guy we had been living with.

We moved to a farm in St. Clair, Michigan, which I was extremely excited about since I had wanted to be farmer so badly. Our house was surrounded by corn fields on all sides and we had so much room to run around and just be kids. I would run through the corn field pretending to be a big John Deere combine harvesting corn and would inspect them to ensure it was the best crop to sell. I started third grade and began the routine of making new friends, learning the area, and unpacking my toys and clothes. This move felt different. This house had a much more somber feeling than the other places we had lived. When I spent the night at Grandma and Papa's house, I was tucked in and told "Goodnight, don't let the bed bugs bite". At my Uncle Tony and Aunt Carrie's house it was the same; complete with a bowl of cereal we called a

Decisions

"midnight snack". My uncle and I would eat Cheerios, talk Detroit Tigers' baseball, and speculate on who would win the "big one". Tigers' baseball is and always will be a favorite pastime, which is fitting since my dad and Uncle Tony were both my little league coaches. At home I felt the complete opposite of how a visit with my aunt and uncle, or my grandparents made me feel. Home life meant lying awake at night hearing my mom and new step-dad scream at each other, not knowing if it was my fault or what they were so angry about. I was almost through third grade when we were evicted from the St. Clair farm, and were forced to move in with my other pair of grandparents; my mom's parents.

My mom's dad was a man who commanded respect. Grandpa G was a well-dressed, well kept, respectable, Polish, man of the Lord. We moved into my grandparents' basement with eight weeks left of my third grade year. I finished third grade at a new school, and decided I was done trying to make new friends. What was the point of meeting new people when I wasn't sure how long we would be living there? My cousin, TJ, moved into my grandparents' house, too, and we became even closer than we already were. TJ and I have that kind of relationship where we can "clown" on each other, and in the same moment feel a deep sympathy if one of us gets hurt. We were the ones who would make decisions on impulse; almost always having made the wrong decision. I always looked up to him, followed him everywhere, and wanted to be just like him. He was the Guess and I.O.U Jeans wearing guy with spiked hair, was flashy, and a smooth talker, while I was the poor kid that wore Bugle Boy, shopped at Kmart, and rode a Schwinn bike. My mom was furious that summer because TJ and I thought it would be entertaining to pedal our bikes as fast as we

5

could and then slam his back tire pegs into the front spokes of my bike tire. That caused my bike to stop abruptly, throwing me over the handle bars while breaking a few spokes each time. My mom spanked my butt so hard that it actually hurt to sit down because by the end of the summer, my front rim was so misshapen, dented, and mangled. TJ and I would go on to discover throughout our teenage years just how many stupid ideas we could come up with.

The living arrangement at my grandparents' house was not ideal to say the least. My mom, step-dad, younger sister, and I lived in the basement, while my older sister slept in an upstairs spare bedroom. My mom's brother, TJ's dad also named Tony, lived there at the same time as we did in another upstairs spare bedroom. I think what made it feel weird, for me, was that my grandparents' house was the place where we spent every Christmas Eve. It's a tradition every year to spend Christmas Eve with my mom's side of the family. We would all go to my grandparents' house for dinner, which took place in their finished basement, where we happened to be living at the time. The decorations would stay up all year long, but would come alive that night as we celebrated another year together. Grandpa G with his Christmas music on the radio, whiskey and water in hand, would tell us grandkids to "Wait awhile" when asking to open presents; that was his answer for everything, "Wait awhile." Growing up in a Polish family, we had strict traditions and were raised Roman Catholic. Christmas Eve night was the time we would exchange the Oplatek, which is a thin wafer made of flour and water, similar in taste to the hosts that are used for communion during Catholic mass. The Christmas wafer is shared before Wigilia, which is the Polish Christmas Eve dinner. This wonderful

Decisions

moment of tradition was now replaced with arguing and turmoil.

After a few short months, at the end of that summer after completing third grade, we moved again. We moved into a three bedroom, ranch style house where I finally had my own room and my two sisters had to share. I had spent almost four months sleeping on a couch in my grandparents' basement, so having my own room felt liberating. I now had my own space to play in, but also to hide. At this point I'm starting fourth grade, all the while expecting we'd only be here in this house for a year before having to move somewhere else, yet again. However, mom told us "This is it, last move." I wanted to believe it; I wanted to have faith in my mom who was desperately juggling a job, three kids, a rocky marriage, and more bills and debt than anyone should have. My step-dad had some sort of disability that rendered him unable to work, so my mom took care of all of us. My older sister would help clean or cook and I helped out where I could. During this period, I saw panic on my mom's face for the first time in my life and I suddenly felt an extreme sense of urgency come over me. I had to do something. Mom was always trying to do what she thought was best for us and I wanted ever so badly to help somewhere, so I started shoveling snow. The great thing about Michigan is there are definitely four seasons which makes it very easy to find seasonal work if you're willing to put forth the effort. I cut grass in the spring and summer and raked leaves in the fall, but the money maker was shoveling snow. I felt like a kid in a candy store one winter when I earned sixty dollars shoveling snow for hours around the neighborhood. I couldn't wait to rush home and show mom what I had done for the family. She was so ecstatic and grateful, she hugged me as tight as she could and thanked me for my hard work. The one thing Mom always taught me was the value of a dollar and the hard work it takes to earn it. My work ethic came mostly out of necessity, but I was lucky enough to have family members that would teach us to work hard, do well in school, and stay out of trouble.

We lived in this house for three years, and during these three years I learned a lot about trust. I was always taught to be honest because life will always be worse if you lie. In life, you will find it's hard to put trust in someone who doesn't reciprocate the same values. One day, I returned home from school to find my step-dad wiping a white powder off of the living room coffee table. I was just a fifth grader, what did I know other than *Gilligan's Island, G.I Joe, Teenage Mutant Ninja Turtles,* and *Golden Girls*? When I asked what the white powder was, I received what could only be described as feeling a thousand pound hand strike my face. My step-dad smacked me so hard that I felt dizzy and my face felt hot to the touch. He told me that if I told my mom, he would beat me harder. That was the first of many beatings I would receive at the hands of guy who I thought loved and cared for us. Boy was I wrong.

A few months later, the fighting between my mom and step-dad went from behind closed doors, to fighting in front of us kids. The panic I witnessed on my mom's face before was now replaced with fear, sadness, and desperation. My mom had this beautiful gold necklace that had mine and my sisters' birthstones inside a set of gold baby bootie charms, which came up missing. I had friends over from school that day doing homework and working on a project together. When my mom got home from work she searched for the necklace, but couldn't find it. Again, it was assumed that it was my fault because I had friends over. Needless to say, my step-dad blamed me

Decisions

for the necklace being stolen. Next thing I know, the cops are involved and my friends are being investigated. The incident reached some other kids at school and I was instantly known as "the kid who called the cops on his friends". Although my friends and I had nothing to do with the missing necklace, it didn't matter to anyone. Therefore, the few friends I did have ended up turning against me. It was discovered a short time later that my step-dad stole the necklace to buy drugs and alcohol.

The fighting between my mother and my step-dad continued and quickly escalated. I remember waking up one night to screaming and banging. I walked out of my room to find my mom pinned up against the wall in the kitchen. My older sister was trying to call 911, but my step-dad had the phone cord wrapped around his hand while pulling it back so she couldn't dial. Mom was yelling at him to let it go, and at the same time, trying to push him off of her. There was so much going on that I couldn't process the gravity of the situation happening all at once. I felt helpless watching my mom stuck in between my sister and this guy who is filled with an enormous amount of rage, not knowing if he was going to hurt them. I remember yelling at the top my lungs then frantically ran into my room to find my wooden Little League baseball bat. I always kept it close by because I never knew if he was going to storm into my room while I was sleeping, having remembered something I had done wrong a few hours before and decided I needed to be disciplined at that very moment. I felt a relief as I quickly retrieved the bat from under my bed and ran into the kitchen, only to find that he now had his hands gripped around mom's neck and shoulder as she's hitting him in the head with the phone in order to break free from his overpowering clutches. My older sister was pushing him away, and while this was happening, I mustered up all the courage I could to swing my bat just like I had practiced for my games. I didn't know where to aim or what impact it would have on the situation unfolding. I was so afraid that my older sister and mother were being harmed, but was also torn over the fact that the man hurting them was supposed to be a father figure and a role model to us. Why would he hurt the ones he is supposed to love? Why would anyone treat someone so badly, and physically cause them so much pain? I swung that wooden bat like I was Kirk Gibson hitting a home run in the 1984 World Series. It was as if he was made of stone; the bat bounced off his hip and this tower of a man grabbed me and threw me to the kitchen floor with such force. Full of terror, I ran to my room and hid underneath my covers crying out to anyone for help.

What took place next would be a defining moment in our lives. The sound of brakes squealing and the howl of sirens brought a sense of security I had not felt in some time. I tiptoed out of my room and peeked around the corner to see the police handcuffing and escorting my step-dad out of the house. It would be a few days before we saw him again. The weight of scared, sleepless nights seemed to escape along with the fear and anxiety of walking home from school not knowing what type of mood he would be in. All these horrible feelings were taken away accompanied by the guy who constantly hurt our family. My mom sat my sisters and me down and talked to us about how sorry she was and that things would change. For the first time in a few years, it was nice to come home from school and not anticipate any kind of verbal abuse which was usually followed by some form of physical abuse. This would be short lived as he returned days later. To say this was unexpected would be an understatement. The only thought that ran through my

Decisions

head was "I am a dead man." I was used to hearing that, but this time, I really felt like my life was over. See, while he was gone, I drank a few of his cans of pop because I figured he wasn't coming back. He drank a lot of Squirt and I decided to drink a few without anyone knowing. My fears were confirmed when I came home and was greeted with a glare from him that was so intense it could melt ice in the middle of a snow storm. I was yelled at for drinking his pop, spanked repeatedly, and sent to my room. I was relieved that evening when mom came home from work because I knew she would not accept what he did to me earlier that day, and would definitely not go unnoticed. Instead, my feeling of relief abruptly turned to disappointment when she yelled at me because I should have known better and those were not mine to drink. Something I thought to be as insignificant as a few sodas suddenly became a huge issue with him and for a while I was constantly reminded by him that I was a thief.

The tension and hostility would once again pick up steam, happening more frequently, culminating with me waking up one night bawling uncontrollably. The few days leading up to this moment I felt like I could do nothing right. I was nitpicked on about everything, even being told if I didn't listen I was a dead man. One day, I was late coming home from a friend's house and when I walked in the door I was told "You're dead." I was awakened a few nights later bawling because I dreamt I had actually died. I was so afraid of not knowing where we went after we died, I was unbelievably terrified. I was shaking, unable to get the thoughts of leaving my mom behind out of my mind, and what would happen next. I was told so many times that if I didn't do something I was a "dead man", and it would eventually consume my every thought. I felt a blanket of heat wrap around my whole body and before I knew it, my mom was comforting me trying her best to calm me down. She said I had a long time before I had to worry about any of that and I should just enjoy being a kid. Considering my upbringing as a Catholic, I understood what death was and that I would go to heaven, but the thought of whether it was true or not was scary and overwhelming. I was sent to bed without feeling any better, still having an abundance of questions swirling around in my head. I spent the next month and a half wrestling with this fear unable to come to terms with our inevitable fate.

My sisters and I returned home one weekend from a regularly scheduled visitation with our father. As we walked through the front door, there was a silence in the house that felt very eerie to me. Our step-dad looked up from his half smoked Newport cigarette with a blank stare on his face. When we asked where mom was, he didn't say a word. He just flicked the ash off the end of his cigarette, looked up at us, and then turned the TV channel as if nothing was wrong. We walked to the back of the house and found our mom sitting in her bedroom by herself. The three of us wrapped our arms around her wondering what happened while we were away. She was crying while telling us she loved us very much. These days, it seemed that's all my mother did was cry. I remember waking up to them fighting and her crying as she locked herself in the bathroom. She would cry harder as he hit her for getting in his business when talking to friends. It seemed that no one was safe from the wave of terror that would come over the house after a heavy night of drinking. A few more fights and a few more 911 calls later, we would never see him again. My family came over and helped my mom, my sisters, and I move back into my grandparents' basement, again. At least now we would be

Decisions

safe and we all looked forward to picking up the pieces of our broken life and putting it back together.

"It's the place people go to escape, a place made of cabins, pine trees and lakes, but no matter how far you drive there's no sign to say "You've Arrived". So just follow your heart till you find...Your special place that brings peace of mind as you breathe in the air and unwind...Your cares are all left behind. It's no mystery where the north woods start. When you arrive Up North you'll know in your heart.
-Suzanne Kindler-

"The effect you have on other people is the greatest currency in the world."
— Jim Carrey, Actor/Comedian -

"But let all who take refuge in you be glad; let them ever sing for joy. Spread your protection over them that those who love your name may rejoice in you."
— Psalm 5:11 —

THE STRUGGLE OF WHO'S WHO 2

Have you ever looked at a picture, heard a song, or smelled something that reminded you of a wonderful place or a funny memory? Is there a time or place in your life that you would like to travel back to and spend just a few more minutes reliving that moment, just soaking up the atmosphere around you? I found a picture from when I was five years old fishing with my father in the back of Papa's farm. There was a lake in the back that my grandparents' and I used to take a walk to and fish. It seemed so peaceful; the birds chirping, the slow breeze coming in across the water, and the smell of flowers in the air. My sisters and I were always asking Papa if we could "go out back." Going out back meant feeding the horses, seeing the pheasants, and helping Papa hammer nails into scrap wood left over from his projects. It was our way of spending good quality time with him, which he loved. He is a strong, but soft spoken southern man from Jellico, Tennessee. Every time I did something foolish, he would always say, "Boy, I tell you what..." Something I have never understood, but like, about southern folks is how relaxed and calm they carry themselves. At Grandma and Papa's house, there was no yelling, cursing, or carrying on. When you walked into the breezeway, the smell of the

Decisions

farm would permeate from the rubber boots over in the corner. That's the smell that brings me back. I loved spending every moment I could at their house. It was warm, loving, and full of wonder like waking up on Christmas morning. There was always something to do, something to discover, plus my sisters and I loved the Sunday family dinners.

My sisters and I spent every other weekend with my father as part of the divorce agreement with my mother. I would spend the next 17 years getting to know my father one weekend at a time. At first, we would stay at Grandma and Papa's house all weekend since that's where my father was living. I used to listen to Papa's Johnny Horton records all the time. Between Johnny Horton and Marty Robbins, both artists' songs had a sense of adventure that I loved right from the start. Songs have meaning, feeling, comfort, adventure, and sorrow. They can be uplifting when you're feeling down, or soothe a broken heart after a loss. Songs have a way of captivating us into their tune and whisking us away in their lyrics.

My dad's youngest brother, my Uncle Derek, is a one of a kind. He and my Aunt Hope lived just a short distance down the road from Grandma and Papa's house in New Haven, MI. It was amazing, the fights my sisters and I would have over who's spending the night at which family member's house. Who's staying at whose house? Who's spending our time with which aunt and uncle? Each one possessed amazing qualities; we always looked forward to spending time with all of them. Aunt Hope was the biggest KISS fan I knew, and Uncle Derek was a volunteer fireman. Uncle Tony was my little league coach with my dad and we spent hours talking baseball, looking at baseball cards, and listening to Marty Robbins records. My dad was my little coach and was also in the military.

Decisions

Growing up, my mom would constantly tell us kids how our father left us and how bad he was. When we were with him, however, it didn't seem like he thought that we were a burden, as it was said to me so many times. I remember I wanted to go with my step-dad and our neighbors on a fishing trip. The trip was on one of the weekends that I was supposed to visit with my dad. When my mom informed my dad that I that I would be going on this trip, I could see the hurt in his eyes. To make matters worse, we told him right after my baseball game he was coaching. He then proceeded to throw his clipboard in the air in disgust. I broke down crying because I was upset that I had hurt my father, but I also didn't want to disappoint my step-dad and our neighbors. How crazy is it that I would think so highly of anybody else and put those people before my own father? Young minds are extremely impressionable and will believe almost anything if told enough times by those closest to us. My dad had asked me if that was what I really wanted and I didn't even know what to say. It is hard being in the middle of two parents whom you do not want to let down, especially knowing that you are in fact about to hurt one of them. In the end, I went on that fishing trip. When we make those hard decisions, there's a transaction taking place; we're trading one for the other. I chose to go on a fishing trip rather than honoring my father and spending time with him. I traded my father's feelings for someone else's.

When I met my wife, she had a three year old son from a previous relationship. When we got married, I was really scared that I would end up being the step parent I dealt with as a child. It's a delicate balance between the father and the new parent. I hated when people would put my father down. What evidence did I have to prove them wrong? The only time that was ever spent with my

Decisions

father was every other weekend and two weeks in the summers. How did I know how he felt and how he thought about us? He always hugged us and told us he loved us very much, that's how. He always treated us with respect and would take us out places. Sometimes in life, examples of behavior are presented to us in different forms that we tend to throw away as irrelevant. Years later, I'm a step parent to a four year old boy and had no idea how I was supposed to act. I was told my whole life that my father walked out on us and he didn't want us. Who doesn't want their children? It seemed as if my father genuinely cared about me, or why else would he take an interest in being my baseball coach? The male role models I had in my life were a guy who beat my mom, my father who left to pursue a career in the military, two uncles who I knew cared a lot about us and tried to teach us right from wrong, and two grandfathers with contrasting parenting styles. Who was I supposed to look up to? The only one I had spent a significant amount of time with was the guy that beat my mom, and I knew I didn't want to be like him. A father is a very important part of a child's life. I've learned that the worst thing you can do is keep a father away from their child who actually wants to be involved their life. I always felt as though my dad could have done more, or showed more, but I always thought maybe he was just a victim of circumstance. Are you a product of your decisions, or a product of your circumstances?

My step-dad wasn't the only step-parent I had growing up. I have had another step parent in my life ever since shortly after my parents divorced. My dad remarried a younger woman, who also had a young girl from a previous marriage. She was awesome, at first. We laughed, sang, acted silly, and joked around a lot. That all

Decisions

changed when my half-sister was born. I was happy and she was great to be around. Between my sisters, step-sister, and now a half-sister, being the only boy would prove to be quite the daunting task. My dad and step-mom moved into a modular home in a trailer park that had a lot of other kids in the neighborhood. On the visitation weekends with my dad it was nice to get out and see those other friends we made in the new neighborhood. There were two other boys living across the street from my dad so it felt great to talk to someone other than girls. I saw how the other kids' fathers acted with them, how my dad acted with me, and how my step-dad acted while saying my father was no good. It was a very confusing and turbulent time in my life. I wished so bad to have a father that loved me and wanted me. One night, I overheard a phone conversation between my mom and dad. My mom was telling my dad that he needed to be more involved in mine and my sisters' lives because we came first. According to my mom, my dad didn't care because he said he now has another family to worry about. Were we being replaced? Did he love those other kids more than us? Did he really leave because he didn't want us, like my mom had always told us? So many nights I cried myself to sleep, wanting answers to these questions.

My step mom did take us places when we visited. We would go to the mall, go out to lunch, or go to the pool. The best part of going on the visitation weekend was ordering pizza and watching the Friday line up of shows, called "TGIF." We would also rent movies from the video store, which was great because we would pop some popcorn and watch some scary movie my dad would picked out. My dad and step-mom would always set aside time to let us pick out movies and watch them with us.

Decisions

Back at home, my step-dad had control of the TV most of the time which meant we never really had the chance to watch that much of what we liked. I would always look forward to visitation weekends because we would get to do so many fun things and weren't constantly spanked or yelled at.

Like the saying goes, "All good things must come to an end." The visitation weekends didn't seem as fun anymore. My dad and step-mom would fight for no reason. I always thought it was because we were there and might have been a burden on them. My step-mom bought me a Jacksonville Jaguars coat because the jacket I was wearing wasn't an appropriate thickness for Michigan winter weather. Later that same weekend, they started fighting and she took the coat back from me. I couldn't believe this was happening, here at a place that I always thought was safe. Eventually, she gave the coat back, but it hurt so much to think that I was the reason my other parents were fighting. During one instance, the fighting was so intense that my sisters and I were hiding next to the couch. My step-mom took off her wedding ring and threw it at my dad's chest. Surrounded by so much anger, at home as well as at my dad's house, I would always ask to stay at Uncle Tony's, Uncle Derek's, or Grandma and Papa's. Those were the three houses I felt the safest, and knew I wouldn't hear screaming and arguing unless it was one of us cousins fighting over a toy. By my teenage years, I had been subjected to so much pain, I never knew who to trust, who was going to leave, or who to turn to for help. Living in constant fear is the worst way to live your life. By the time I felt comfortable at one my relatives' houses, it was time to go back home to a house of spankings and emotional abuse. I'm not saying spankings are good or bad, but not everything a child does requires a leather belt or wooden paddle across the butt, slapped in the mouth, or put in a corner all the time. I learned to follow the rules out of fear rather than out of respect or knowledge. I've tried to teach my kids rather than beat them into submission, or continuously yell at them every day all day, but it's not easy. I've witnessed enough examples of bad parenting to last me a lifetime; by no means did I want to add to that list when I became a father, so I have had to work hard every day to break the cycle. My mom would tell us stories about how Grandpa used to make her kneel on rice, and beat them with leather belts. My sisters and I would always get threatened if we didn't do our chores, clean our rooms, or step out of line. Obeying out of fear rather than respect is the fastest way to ruin your child's chances of becoming an effective parent.

Trust always seems to be an issue in relationships whether it is between spouses, couples, or between parents and children. I find it fascinating how mean we can be to our loved ones, but then turn around and hold the door open for a complete stranger, or talk nice about someone we barely know. My wife and I would fight about everything. She grew up in an environment similar to mine. We weren't showing each other respect, which meant we didn't have respect for the relationship itself. That behavior manifested into cheating allegations, yelling, fighting, and it was as though I was reliving everything I grew up around. My worst fear was coming true; I was losing my wife and kids. I used to ask my mom for marriage advice, but then I realized, why am I asking someone with two divorces for marriage advice? Bad idea. That's like asking someone who's bankrupt for financial advice on how to be a millionaire. You just never know the effect your words and actions will have on someone else.

Decisions

The more broken promises there are, the less love there is, and resentment begins to build. I cared about everyone, but the more I was disappointed the less I cared. There were a few times I would go with my step-dad out to see his friends. I'm not sure if it's because I wanted to go or because my mom had hoped if I was there maybe he wouldn't make any bad decisions. A few days before I left with my dad, I was promised a Nintendo Gameboy if I didn't tell my mom where my step-dad and I had been and what items he bought and picked up. I remember sitting in the car on the floor boards in front of his friend's house because it wasn't safe for kids to be there. My step-dad had told me to hide on the floor, don't look out the windows, and don't open the car doors for anyone. It felt like I had been there forever which started to scare me because I would hear voices of people walking by the car, but I knew I wasn't allowed to look. A while later, he returned to the car to find me crying and told me "Suck it up, you're fine." I was on the floor of a car, in the dark, in a very dangerous part of the city of Detroit infested with drugs and gangs at thirteen years old, but promised I would never say anything to my mother. He promised me that game system would be waiting for me in my room when I returned home from the visitation weekend with my dad, but it wasn't there. I never did get anything he ever promised me.

Who's who? Who do I go to with problems when everything around me is dark? I kept hearing negativity about both sides of the family; Mom and step-dad talk bad about dad, step-mom talks bad about mom and step-dad, Dad throws his two cents in every now and then as well. Aunt and uncles have their comments and opinions, and us kids involved are torn to pieces. I carried around so much anger, so much hurt, so much confusion that when I

Decisions

became a teenager and was going into my twenties, the relationships I had were not healthy. It was all about what I wanted in the relationship. I never took the time to care about what the other person wanted. What I wanted always outweighed what my girlfriends wanted or cared about. With enough bad examples I was forced to figure all this out on my own.

So, who's who? If my dad is so bad, and my mom is so bad, who do I go to? My step-dad went to jail one more time and that was the opening my mother needed to finally break the chains of abuse, and we moved back to my grandparents' house. I remember sitting up late talking to my grandfather about how I was feeling and if God was so merciful then why would he let all these bad things happen? This started my questioning of the Catholic religion. We were raised strict Roman Catholic and I couldn't understand where God was during all this. My grandfather helped me through these issues and signed me up for the Columbian Squires. Grandpa was part of a Catholic fraternal organization called the Knights of Columbus. All the adult members would have monthly meetings and give back to the community. The Squires is the young men's version of the Knights of Columbus. I joined when I was thirteen and I was instantly hooked. We would attend Detroit Tigers' baseball games for our sports outing, camping and canoeing for our summer outing, snowboarding in the winter and retreats throughout the year. I enjoyed it so much that I ran for board positions and was the third highest ranking member in the state of Michigan. My grandfather knew I needed an outlet and this outlet would bring me closer to God. I don't know where I would have been without him. Grandpa G sadly passed away in 2013 due to an inoperable brain tumor.

Decisions

Living with my grandparents had its ups and down. Some of the funniest memories I have, come from when my sisters, TJ, and I would make voice recordings my younger sister's first Sony tape recorder. We would tell jokes and act silly on these tapes and it would drive my grandparents crazy. I think it's the moments that we either upset someone or share in their joy that make certain memories more prominent than others. My grandfather had to sit in *his* chair, drink from *his* coffee cup, and use *his* fork. If someone was using one of his items, he would take it from you, or make you go wash it because it was *his*. He had this fork that had a big bend in the prongs with a distinct design on the handle. His coffee cup was the same; it had a special design and it was his to drink black coffee out of. Those little ticks a person has can stick with us forever and bring us back into a time that was special to us, or was better than where we are now. When life gets chaotic, we need these memories to bring us back to center.

What is your center? Have you ever thought about defining a tether? Most married couples will say it's each other, but what happens when you are fighting? You're destroying your center instead of using it to calm you down. My wife and kids are at my center, my grandfather, memories from different happy times in my life, and my Lord and Savior are at my center. Think about a kite flying in the wind and you're at the other end of the string; the tether. What tethers you, what anchors you down when the weight of the world starts to overtake your life? Craft yourself a spiritual reminder to aid you in tethering yourself. My spiritual reminder is Jeremiah 29:11. I love that bible passage about how God knows the plans for you. I don't know what God has planned for me, but it's exciting to find out. However, it can also be very scary because maybe we're not sure if we're on the right track and actually following God's will for us. If you're not religious, that's fine. You'll find out later on about my battle with religion, addiction, and eventually my self-destructive downward spiral to rock bottom. The spiritual reminder is a sentence or a phrase that brings everything back into alignment. Sometimes we say "It is what it is", "Everything happens for a reason", "Let the good times roll", and the list of quotes goes on. It doesn't have to be gimmicky or something everyone knows, but think about a phrase or something you can say or think about to help bring you back to center. My most wonderful childhood memories of Christmas time was at my grandparents' house for Christmas Eve dinner.

We lived at my grandparents' house for two years in my seventh and eighth grade years. During that time, there was healing and restoration taking place. We could finally live our lives in peace, and not fear. I spent a lot of nights sitting at the kitchen table with my grandfather trying to figure out why we were living the way we were. I saw so many happy people doing just fine, but here we were living in my grandparents' basement again. I was attending my sixth school and living in my fifth house. Why would God do this to us? We went to church every Sunday and I was involved in a Catholic youth organization. What were we doing wrong? My grandfather would tell me not to worry and that God was preparing us and strengthening us through every situation. God never wastes pain; he uses it to fulfill his plan for us. At this point, I believed anything I could. I stopped making friends; I became like a hermit, and sat in front of the TV all day. I wasn't sure how long we'd be staying here because mom was constantly looking for new places for us to live. You never know what will shake up your life. A

Decisions

phone call, a stranger, something that randomly appears in your life unexplainable can seem like a blessing, but quickly turn out to be nothing more than a disaster. Sometimes, it happens right in your own backyard, literally.

My mother received a phone call one day about a van she was selling. A Man called wanting to meet to see the van and talk about the price. Shortly into the meeting, he made it aware to my mother that he wasn't interested in the van at all, but in fact, interested in her. It turned out he lived right behind us and his backyard shared the same fence as my grandparents'. Two years after the hell we lived through, there is now another guy entering our lives? He seemed nice enough and was genuinely polite. He was originally from up north near the Port Sanilac area where his parents lived on a farm with a decent amount of property. My mother decided to start a relationship with him and after a while, decided to have us move into his house. We moved in right behind our grandparents' house which was great just in case this situation turned out like the past. My sisters now had rooms of their own, and guess where I slept? You guessed it, I lived in the basement. These houses all had finished basements so it was pretty nice. He made it comfortable and I was able to have my own space until someone would come down to do laundry. It was a small sacrifice in order to have your own space and live in peace, or so we thought.

This new guy was raised on a farm and had a very strict work ethic. He used to get extremely upset with me for sleeping until 10am on a Saturday because according to him, I should have been up at dawn. I was starting my freshman year of high school and was stressed out about that change, so I slept a little later. He felt there was always something to do around the house, there's no time for relaxation, and the weekends are the time to work, not have fun. I felt this new guy was always trying to push his beliefs and values on us and I didn't always agree with his thinking. I already had a pretty good work ethic because I had examples from my mother, grandfather, and other family members that worked very hard to achieve their goals. We are all different, and trying to make someone else believe what you believe can ruin a relationship. Having respect for the relationship means accepting their values and beliefs without competing or forcing yours on them.

The new guy would take me up to his parents' farm sometimes. I told them about how I dreamed of becoming a farmer ever since I was a toddler and how I talked myself out of it because equipment was so expensive. Have you ever talked yourself out of following a dream? Have you talked yourself out of achieving a goal? There's a transaction taking place in that internal dialogue about why you should or shouldn't follow your dream. If you talked yourself out of achieving something, you just bought into those reasons. You're selling yourself, or someone else, on the reasons why you should or shouldn't make that decision. You either buy into the reasons, or you don't. When a car salesman is selling you a car, he talks about how great it is and how easy it is for you to afford. Only you know your situation. You either buy the car because of the salesman's reasons, or buy the car because it's what you want. Maybe you don't buy the car because it's not something you want, either way, there's a transaction taking place. I sold myself the reasons why I shouldn't follow my dream and bought into it. My advice is to buy into your dreams no matter what. Buy into your vision, buy into your goals and OWN it! The new guy's parents gave a lot of pros and cons about the farming

Decisions

business. In the end, I chose not to pursue becoming a farmer, although, I have had many gardens in the places I lived, so in a sense I did complete my goal but on a much smaller scale. It's all about perspective.

While we were up at his parents' house, we would ride four-wheelers, shoot guns, go hunting, and chop wood. I learned a lot about living in the country and the values his family had. My dad, Uncle Tony, and Uncle Derek all taught me how to shoot guns, and a bow and arrow. We would shoot at Grandma and Papa's house on the Sundays we were visiting. I was really good, but according to the new guy, whoever taught me must have "sucked". I told him my dad taught me and he said "Yeah, since he takes such an interest in your life." My first thought was, "Who are you, and what do you know?" All he knew was what my mother may have told him, he had no firsthand knowledge. I was faced with yet another person talking about someone I cared about. My dad isn't perfect, but he is still my dad and I love him. From this moment forward, I was very guarded around the new guy due to the fact that I felt like history was starting to repeat itself. I had no idea what lie ahead.

When I told mom what he had said, at first, she didn't believe me. I told her he was talking bad about my dad and I didn't like it, and I definitely don't want to be in another situation like before. I told her that we didn't need him, especially if he's going to be mean. She said that she would talk to him about it and not to worry. I *was* worried though, because we had only known him for a few months before we moved in and we were still in the process of feeling out the situation. We were learning each other's ticks and what made everyone mad.

A couple weeks later, it's football season. Who doesn't love football on Sunday and the food that goes with it? The new guy didn't like sports, at all. Fishing, hunting, camping, building things, and chopping wood was what he loved best. I do like those things, but not every day, week, or month. In Detroit, we watch Tigers' baseball from spring to fall, then onto Lions' football, and lastly Red Wings' hockey in the winter. I had played baseball and hockey since the second grade and it is an enormous part of my life. Living at the new guy's house, if you didn't like what he liked, or believed what he believed to be right or wrong, it would quickly escalate to an argument.

That year, Bret Favre took the Green Bay Packers to the Super Bowl. My mom and I were pretty happy because not only are the Packers in the Lions' division, but we know a few friends that are fans. However, that day the new guy said I HAD to work with him in the garage building something he needed. I told him I wanted to watch the Super Bowl; he then said that he didn't care what I wanted. My mom got involved and told him I could help until it was time to watch the game. I helped him for a few hours until the game started, but he kept saying "A little bit longer", "...a little bit longer." I went inside to get a drink and to catch the score of the game. As I was standing in the kitchen next to the door leading to the garage, he came inside and said that I needed to get back in to help, and he grabbed my shirt collar and yanked me back into the garage. I immediately spun around, pushed him off, and screamed "Get off of me! You're not my father!" Well, there are two problems with this scenario; 1) I was living in *his* house 2) In order to respect my mother, I can't cause issues within their relationship. Luckily, my mother saw what had happened and yelled at him, and then explained all that we had been through and she will not put up with it again. Towards the end of the school year, my older sister graduated high school and the

<u>Decisions</u>

fighting between my mom and her now ex-boyfriend, and him and me, intensified. My Sister moved out to get away from him, which caused my mom to end the relationship and we moved again. I'm not sure what's worse; the physical abuse or the emotional abuse. The physical wounds will heal, but what about the emotional scars left behind? My mother bought a house about an hour out of the city, only about a half hour away from my Grandma and Papa's house, which was great. We were forced to move for what would be the last time before I graduated high school. Yet again, I would have to start over at another school and meet new people, and be the new guy. At least it would be for the last time.

"God never wastes your pain. Just because you don't see me smiling, doesn't mean I'm not okay...Maybe I'm just focused on how God is going to use my pain to help somebody get through what I've already been through."
- Stan Williams, U.S. Air Force Veteran/Motivational Speaker/Author -

Decisions

"Do not let your hearts be troubled. Believe in God, believe also in me. In my Father's house there are many dwelling places. If it were not so, would I have told you that I go to prepare a place for you? And if I go and prepare a place for you, I will come again and will take you to myself, so that where I am, there you may be also. And you know the way to the place where I am going. Thomas said to him, 'Lord, we do not know where you are going. How can we know the way?' Jesus said to him, 'I am the way, and the truth, and the life. No one comes to the Father except through me. If you know me, you will know my Father also. From now on you do know him and have seen him.'"
- John 14:1-7 –

THE PERECT FIT
3

Where do you fit in? What group of people do you feel most comfortable with? High school....some people say it's the best four years of your life. Some say it's an experience you will never forget. Others hated high school and couldn't wait to leave. I say high school might be the worst time of a teenager's life. There are so many changes happening during those four years, it can be scary. A support system should definitely be in place and some patience would come in handy as well. This is the time where the sports start playing a big role, you should start being intentional about your future, and an ugly epidemic will rear its head.

I had played baseball and hockey every year until I turned 18. When I got into high school I decided to try football, which was a huge mistake. I'm not sure who else agrees, but in my high school there were the "preps", the "nerds", the "freaks", the "loners", and the "jocks". There are two types of "jocks": the football jocks and everyone else. For some reason, the football players were the ones who got all the girls, were the most popular, but yet the biggest bullies in the entire school. Where I lived was the cliché small town where football was important and the football players were even more important. I was friends with some baseball players and some wrestlers, but when I was on the football team it was ruthless, and that's putting it lightly. This false sense of brotherhood ran through the locker room and I saw some respectable young men get hazed and picked on. I knew it wasn't for me, but I was on the team and the association alone was enough for me to be grouped into the popular crowd. I felt like if I could get into the group everyone looked up to, I would get the same attention. I couldn't have been more wrong!

I attended freshman year at one high school while we lived with mom's ex-boyfriend and then attended the next three years of high school at another school when we moved up north out of the city. This was a huge culture shock as the sidewalks are rolled up, so to speak, around 6pm daily. Unless you had a license or lived in the country with some property, life was very boring. The main difference was the focus was on the football team, and not so much on the other sports. There wasn't much access to hockey teams or baseball teams unless it was sponsored through the school. Idle hands are the devil's playground and that's how it usually starts. I don't like to sit and do nothing, which is why I fill my calendar with things to do. I don't like to feel like I'm wasting my life away watching TV, playing video games, or anything else but accomplishing my goals and getting ahead in life. I've had enough examples in my life of people who weren't following their dreams, weren't living out their values, and wasting their life away. Your values are where you want to be in life, the goals are the accomplishments along the way. I have a lot of goals and my values are attached to those goals. That's what I call "Living Your Brand". You live your brand when you live out your values with a genuine heart. If you say honesty is your value but lie to everyone, you're not living your brand. If you say family is your value, but yet you're physically abusing your spouse and children, you're not living out your values. "Live Your Brand"; live out your

Decisions

values every day and never let anyone deter you from being who you are.

Bullying is the true epidemic that runs through every school in America. I have seen some kids get beat up, smacked around, and get made fun of for every little thing, which deters them from pursuing any passion they may have. There's a big difference between making fun of your *friends* for doing something stupid or saying something crazy, and a complete other to push a kid down and call him names or shove him in a locker. I'm not innocent by any means, I did stupid stuff, too, but I wasn't as mean as most of the kids. I was sitting in English class one day and my friend who was sitting next to me got beat up in class. We were sitting quietly working on some school work when out of nowhere a student in front walks to the back and hit my friend so hard he knocked him out of his desk chair. Walking on egg shells anywhere is nerve racking. We were always taught that schools and police officers were always safe, but that doesn't seem to be true anymore. I remember when the Columbine school shooting happened. I kept thinking that someone in our school might have the same idea, and that it could easily happen to any one of us who may have been making fun of someone. All it takes is a wakeup call.

My sophomore year of high school I made a decision. I was not putting up with anyone's crap and I was not going to be mean or bully anyone. This turned out to be an incredibly unpopular decision. When I said "Idle hands are the devil's playground", I'm proof of this. I lived in a very boring, very small town where marijuana was exceedingly rampant. I was friends with a lot of people, but only hung out with a select few. I always kept my circles small because I had major trust issues due to everything I endured up to this point. You quickly find out

Decisions

how fast your so-called "friends" will leave you or stab you in the back if you don't follow their ideas or beliefs. Instead of supporting my decision of not being mean and helping out those who are getting bullied, my friends turned on me. Every day for a week, I was forced to fight off one of my former friends.

The week of my sophomore spring break was one of the worst so far in my life. My friends who I put a lot of trust in and hung around with everyday were now against me for any and every reason they could possibly come up with. The first day, I had told a guy in our group to quit talking bad about this one kid he barely knew. Disagreeing with him in front of our peers did not sit well. After school, a small group of kids had formed around my house as my former friend and I are yelling at each other and arguing about what had transpired earlier at school. Punches were thrown and when the dust settled, he was bleeding and everyone left, unhappy with the result.

The next day, my very good friend came to the house, with an even bigger group. I was in the house doing homework and he came inside yelling at me to get outside and fight him. I told him I was sorry he felt that way and to think about all we had been through together. Nothing I said seemed to matter to him, and after his many attempts to get me angry, he left my house and I looked like a scared little boy in everyone's eyes. When my mom got home from work that day, my younger sister told her what he had done. My mother was very hurt and angry because this was a close friend, the one friend she really liked, cared a great deal for, and she felt disrespected because of how much time he had spent at our house. My mother screamed at me to get in the car and we drove to his house. When we arrived, Mom knocked on the door and explained to his dad the

Decisions

situation. When he came outside his dad asked him if there was a problem between us. Not surprisingly, the answer out of his mouth was "Yes", and when that happened, our parents coerced us to fight. It lasted about 30 seconds when I got him on the ground and was punching him in the back of the head. My mother had to pull me off of him. I was so frustrated with everything that was going on and how my friends, who I deeply cared about, could turn their backs on me. Across the street from his house, another close friend who lived behind me was with our group of friends, and witnessed this all unfolding. I tried to go after them, too, to make a point that I was done dealing with the way they had been treating me.

The next day, I was told I was a "dead man" by the whole group I was formerly a part of. I had heard this so many times in my life up to this point; you could say I was numb to the threats. I went about my day thinking nothing more of it. When I got home from school, my two former friends I fought with the past two days were knocking on my back door. I peeked out the door to see what they wanted and they said that they needed to talk. They were talking about how they were sorry for everything that happened and didn't know why all this started. As I'm listening to the story, the door bursts open with an enormous amount of force, and I was thrown out the door into the backyard. I was set up to get my guard down, and the older guy who was almost graduated from school, had come in and jumped me at my house. Those three made sure I couldn't fight back and I was severely beaten for my transgressions from the past few days. My younger sister had witnessed all this and was taken away by some of the older girls at the house who had come to watch this event. By this time there was a large crowd that gathered around while I was beaten so bad that I couldn't get up off the ground. I remember someone yelling at me to stay down, but I never knew what "staying down" meant. I never gave up and I never quit anything. I surely wasn't going to give up in front of this large group yelling for my demise. Finally, I was knocked unconscious, and the fight was over.

My younger sister and a friend of hers we grew up with found me lying up against one of the pillars supporting the carport. I was bleeding and barely cognizant of what had just occurred. I remember sitting in the kitchen with an ice pack to my face when my mom came home. She was so irate and so scared for my well-being she called the police to file a report. I told her everything that was going on and why things were happening this way while we drove to the hospital. The diagnosis was multiple jaw fractures, concussions, fractured right wrist, and a piece of my lower ear was severely cut that needed to be stitched together. I also had the normal facial bruising and soreness of the ribs and kidneys. I couldn't help but think in that moment that all those times I was spanked and hit as a child maybe somehow strengthened my body for this fight. It's sad to say that I was abused as a kid and this was nothing I wasn't already used to, and I cried the whole way home from the hospital. The worst part was my mom had to wake me up every two hours due to the severity of the concussion, because there was a chance I wouldn't wake up when I went to sleep. I spent my sophomore year spring break healing before returning to school.

Returning to school was extremely awkward. Everyone stared at me like they didn't know who I was. A few people told me how sorry they were that this happened, and one girl even gave me flowers. This was

Decisions

the point where I started making better decisions about who my friends were and what I said and did. This experience allowed me to heal in a lot of different ways. I shed the negativity around me, I gained new friends who I am still friends with today, and I learned about trust. The guy who jumped me wound up arrested on unrelated charges, was sent to jail because of those charges, and also because of what he did to me. I never looked back as I moved through high school.

Going into my junior year, I started playing hockey through a church youth group near my house. I was still in the Squires Youth Group, and it was this group and those close to me that helped me keep it together. I found out a few of them were in this hockey league and I couldn't wait until I could play again. I got my driver's license, I started working, and things were going okay. It was nice not being the new kid anymore and everyone was moving on from what had happened during spring break last year. I still wasn't liked by everyone, but I didn't care. I stopped playing football in school, and concentrated on hockey and baseball. I had a new set of friends and that year turned out to be pretty decent. I can't remember too many out of the ordinary, gut wrenching, problematic situations that I encountered. I even had a new girlfriend and a new car. I paid five hundred dollars for a forest green 1992 Dodge Shadow ES. My dad had a car like this and I was excited to be driving. I could finally venture out, see more people, and go more places now that I could drive. It's funny the lessons you learn when you least expect it. I drove the Shadow until the head gasket blew and was no longer drivable.

My mom bought me another car, a Chrysler Reliant. It reminded me of the car Detective Taggart from The Beverly Hills Cop movie drove. That car didn't last

Decisions

long because a piston rod broke and was shot right through the engine block. My friends and I bought an engine from a salvage yard, replaced the broken engine, and sold the car. Grandpa G's friend let me use a car he had sitting at his auto shop. I was very thankful that my grandfather's friend would let me use one of his cars since I was out of money and my mom was not going to buy me another car. He let me borrow a 1989 Grand Prix, but there was a catch. Every time I turned left with a quarter tank of gas or less, the car would sputter and shut off. It would take a few minutes before the car could restart, and my friends would laugh at me every time. It became a running joke that if we came up to a left turn, everyone in the care would hurry to look at my gas gauge to see if we were going to stall out. I just figured there were some sediments in the tank stopping the fuel pump from getting gas. I called my grandfather's friend and he told me since I was giving it back soon, I didn't need to fix it; just make sure at least above a quarter tank of gas was in the car at all times.

      I feel like we do this a lot in certain areas of our life. I could have fixed all these cars and I would have had a better running vehicle. I chose not to fix the problems and just deal with them until they broke. I never performed any preventative maintenance to ensure everything was running smooth. How many times do we do that in our lives? How many times do we think that it's just easier to deal with the problems instead of fixing them? The saying goes "The grass isn't always greener on the other side." I bet if we watered our side of the fence more often than we do, we wouldn't have to look and wonder what's on the other side of the fence. I could have invested more time and money into the cars, just like I look back and see all the times I could have invested more in my life,

Decisions

relationships, and my performance in my previous jobs. We're always looking for the perfect fit. We constantly change cars, relationships, friendships, jobs, and many other things trying to find the right fit for our lives. More often than not, we end up settling right where we are. I've done this so many times it became more and more common. The doors are there, we just have to have the courage to grab the door knob, give it a turn, and walk through the door of opportunity, promotion, and happiness. I used to look at what everyone else had, what everyone else was doing, instead of being grateful of what I earned or what I had. I became jealous of others' happiness, the cars, houses, money, anything I wanted and someone else had. By counting other people's blessings I was missing the many blessings in my own life. I always felt like I was meant for something great, something bigger than where I currently was. I have always had this burning fire inside that I was going to change the world, change the culture, or change someone's life.

There are two types of people in this world: Thermometers and Thermostats. A thermometer measures the current temperature while thermostats have the ability to establish the temperature, maintain it, or change the temperature. For most of my life, I was just measuring temperature. I would just deal with whatever came my way instead of learning from it and becoming better than I was yesterday. I have learned through many disappointments and missed opportunities that I need to be a thermostat and be intentional on seizing the opportunities presented. I need to water my side of the fence and not worry about what's happening on the other side. I reflect back on relationships that I walked away from instead of investing myself fully. If I didn't like how things were going, instead of fixing the problems and issues, I chose to walk away. I changed jobs frequently citing the fact that I didn't feel fulfilled. I was always looking for something else, the next big thing, and not being grateful or content where I was or what I was doing. The problem with this logic, of course, is you will always be chasing the next big thing and will wind up running around in circles having never felt satisfied. You have to be content where you are now, in order to be satisfied later. I had to learn this principle in order to prioritize my life.

I have always had a lot of dreams and aspirations that I wanted to obtain. Remember, I wanted to be a farmer, but I talked myself out it. My high school years were spent going through the motions because society says that we go to school to get a high school diploma, attend college to get an Associate's Degree or a Bachelors, and settle into corporate America. I didn't have a purpose and I wasn't following a dream. I was going through the motions studying and taking tests, going to work, and waking up doing it over and over again. You have to live on purpose! The worst thing you can do is live out someone else's values, someone else's dreams, or someone else's goals. We all have a purpose for our lives and it's up to us to find it. I have always felt a deep sensing that I had a purpose, but I could never figure out what it was. I'm still not sure I know exactly what my purpose is, but the difference now is that I am more mindful of the opportunities presented and the lessons I've learned along the way. We all fall into constant cognitive traps. We mind read, assume, jump to conclusions, blame ourselves, or blame others for the reasons why we are the way we are. Instead of falling into these traps, be intentional to be better than you were yesterday. If you notice the same things happening every week or every month, maybe you haven't learned the

Decisions

lesson presented. I know for a fact that I've had to repeat the same lessons over and over again because I never learned the first time. I was making the same mistakes again and again and could never figure out why my life wasn't get any better or any different. That's called insanity; doing the same things over and over again expecting a different outcome. Stop being insane, be a thermostat, and change the culture at your job, in your relationships, and in every aspect of your life.

It wasn't until I graduated high school and was working at Discount Tire that I felt the need to change. My mother told me it's time to get serious and figure out what I'm going to do with the rest of my life. I still didn't know, but since I screwed around in high school and barely graduated, I was thinking I would follow my father's footsteps and join the military. I knew that I wanted to join the Air Force or Marine Corps, but I was living at my mom's house and living paycheck to paycheck. My older sister moved out and was in college, my younger sister was a freshman in high school, and I was waking up doing the same thing every day. By this time, I was slowly giving up on faith, giving up on God, and trying to figure things out on my own. This was a definitive turning point in my life where I went wrong. We often make decisions not knowing the implications or the impact our decisions will have on other people.

Now that I was out of high school and 18 years old, I had friends that were over 21. I figured I was an adult; it wouldn't hurt anything if I had a few beers every now and then. Even though my mother told me that alcoholism runs in our family, I always said that it would never happen to me. How many times have we said that or heard that from someone? "It will never happen to me" has gotten a lot of people in trouble, pregnant, alcohol and drug problems, or jail time. After work I'd go to a friend's house a few blocks away from home and drink. I don't know why or how it started, but I was drinking and smoking. At the time I'm sure I had a reason, but years later I really don't know why I ever chose to start. My decisions weren't only impacting me, but I was living at my mom's still, and these weren't exactly the most respectful actions I could display.

One morning, change came unexpectedly. I was talking with some friends about not wanting to spend my whole life working at Discount Tire because it wasn't much of a career. Most of the time, high school kids came to work after school and on the weekends, or the older guys were the managers, so I was stuck somewhere in the middle. After opening one morning, the radio in the shop came alive with panic, excitement, worry, and frantic talking. An airplane had flown into one of the twin towers at the World Trade Center in New York City. Listening to the radio, we could only imagine what was happening on TV and in New York. In Michigan, we have tunnels and bridges that connect to Canada. These paths of transportation were immediately shut down after finding out that this event could possibly be the result of terrorists. This event, known today as "9/11" sent me on the path I'm still following today. I called my dad, who was still in the military, to find out if he was called in. He briefly explained what he could and hung up. The entire country was on alert, and everyone was unsure of where the next target would be, or against whom. This was the push I needed. I had been talking to a recruiter a few months prior to this event about joining the Air Force. That day, I called him and said I wanted to leave ASAP. I found a purpose, I found my why, and I needed to follow it. A few months later, in November 2001, I left for U.S. Air Force Basic Training. I was excited, scared, anxious, and

Decisions

ready for this next adventure. I thought "This is where I'm supposed to be, this is my purpose." My family was very proud of the choice I made, but they also knew the uncertainty of the world during the months after 9/11. I was ready for anything, but I don't think my mother was ready to give up her baby boy. Military forces were being deployed overseas at a rapid rate to combat the terrorists that destroyed the World Trade Center and the Pentagon on September 11th. My mother and I knew the chances of me being sent over to the Middle East after basic training and tech school, but my service to our country outweighed any fear. I have never regretted serving my country and I believe that if 9/11 had never happened, I may not have ever enlisted in the Air Force. We never know where our path may take us, but we must always have the courage to follow it. Stop being afraid of what could go wrong in your life and start being excited about what could go right.

When I was a little boy, I loved putting puzzles together. The blueprint is on the box, and you have to try and recreate that image. I feel that's what God does. We are created in his image, and the puzzle pieces represent moments in our lives. Do you stop building your puzzle because a piece doesn't fit? Think about how puzzles are put together; do you start with the perfect piece? Do you have a system of putting the pieces together?

Life is a giant puzzle God has created for us to build. It's not an image of despair or negativity, but an image of love, hope, and prosperity! What puzzle are you building?

"Never let the things you want make you forget the things you have." – Billy Cox, Expert Keynote Speaker/Author/Sales Trainer/Social Media Strategist -

Decisions

"Finding a perfect fit for yourself is like going through a mountain of keys just to open one lock, you might as well start picking the lock before you lose interest or give up."
- Unknown –

"Surely God is good to Israel, to those who are pure in heart. [2] But as for me, my feet had almost slipped; I had nearly lost my foothold. [3] For I envied the arrogant when I saw the prosperity of the wicked. [4] They have no struggles; their bodies are healthy and strong. [5] They are free from common human burdens; they are not plagued by human ills. [6] Therefore pride is their necklace; they clothe themselves with violence. [7] From their callous hearts comes iniquity; their evil imaginations have no limits. [8] They scoff, and speak with malice; with arrogance they threaten oppression. [9] Their mouths lay claim to heaven, and their tongues take possession of the earth. [10] Therefore their people turn to them and drink up waters in abundance. [11] They say, "How would God know? Does the Most High know anything?" [12] This is what the wicked are like—always free of care, they go on amassing wealth.

[13] Surely in vain I have kept my heart pure and have washed my hands in innocence. [14] All day long I have been afflicted, and every morning brings new punishments. [15] If I had spoken out like that, I would have betrayed your children. [16] When I tried to understand all this, it troubled me deeply [17] till I entered the sanctuary of God; then I understood their final destiny. [18] Surely you place them on slippery ground; you cast them down to ruin. [19] How suddenly are they destroyed, completely swept away by terrors! [20] They are like a dream when one awakes; when

Decisions

you arise, Lord, you will despise them as fantasies.
[21] When my heart was grieved and my spirit embittered,
[22] I was senseless and ignorant; I was a brute beast before
you. [23] Yet I am always with you; you hold me by my right
hand. [24] You guide me with your counsel, and afterward
you will take me into glory. [25] Whom have I in heaven but
you? And earth has nothing I desire besides you. [26] My
flesh and my heart may fail, but God is the strength of my
heart and my portion forever. [27] Those who are far from
you will perish; you destroy all who are unfaithful to you.
[28] But as for me, it is good to be near God. I have made the
Sovereign LORD my refuge; I will tell of all your deeds.
- Psalm 73 –

AND SO IT BEGINS...

4

Have you ever looked back at a moment of your life and said, "Yea that was dumb", or "Hey, remember that one time?" I had a lot of those moments during my life, and even more so during my military career. I enlisted after 9/11 and entered Air Force Basic Training. The hardest part about it was the fact that I graduated the week after Christmas. Christmas for our family means everything. It's the most wonderful time of the year! It's a time for family, food, and most of all, it's the culmination of the entire year, and there's always magic in the air. It was very hard being away from home at 18 during our favorite holiday. All I could think about was my family gathering at my grandparents' house eating ham and homemade pierogi. The best part of our holidays is always the food. Our family cooks some amazing dishes for Thanksgiving and Christmas Eve, and I was stuck in San Antonio, Texas, in basic training. Even thinking about it now, I can't decide if I'm still upset I missed it, or just hungry thinking about the amazing food.

My mom and younger sister came to watch my graduation from basic training. I was so excited to see them, especially since my mom swore she'd never step foot on an airplane. It felt amazing to see both of them

Decisions

after six weeks of being yelled at and having our beds and uniforms thrown around the open bays that we slept in. Basic training was definitely an eye opening experience and I learned a lot about courage, motivation, character, and to never give up. Having my mom and sister with me now was definitely a welcomed sight, and they could see the changes I went through in just six weeks. I could tell by the way they looked at me now how proud they were of me, and I was so happy with the decision I made to join the U.S. Air Force.

After basic training and spending three days with my mom and sister, I was headed to Technical Training at Shephard AFB, Wichita Falls, Texas. I was finally scheduled for class to learn about my job. Each branch has their own acronyms for everything, but in my experience, I would like to say the Air Force has the most. Even the service name is an acronym; AF = Air Force. My AFSC - Air Force Specialty Code - is 2A3X3A, which is a Tactical Aircraft Maintenance Specialist, or Crew Chief on the F-15. I was very excited because out of all the tactical fighter jets I could have worked on, the F-15 was the one I really wanted. Tech school was almost six months long and was a lot of fun. Although I was not thrilled about taking tests, I wasn't trying to fight this process. I had been working on cars most of my life so working with tools and being a mechanic wasn't anything new to me. I couldn't wait to get out of tech school and get to my first duty station to get my hands on some real aircraft.

A couple months into tech training, I was finally allowed to drive. I bought a Mitsubishi Mirage Coupe. I really liked the car. It was small and sporty, and I couldn't wait to customize it to my own personality. I bought engine parts, CD player, speakers, and all the nice stuff I couldn't afford back in high school. I bought the car on a

Decisions

Tuesday and installed everything the next two days in preparation for a trip to Dallas/Fort Worth on Friday. Friday finally came and I was incredibly thrilled to cruise out with some friends to Fort Worth. I was in my car and my two friends were in another car. While on the freeway, it started to rain. Now, I'm getting mad because I spent a lot of time washing and waxing the car so it would look nice just in case I met any girls during the trip. We were having such a good time on the road and we were truly psyched to finally be away from base. At some point, the excitement took over and we were racing each other on the freeway. I know there were a few other cars that were racing, too, so we decided to play along. This scenario was the perfect storm, so to speak. It was at night, raining, and we were racing new cars we weren't yet familiar with. I'm following my friend since he knows where to go, and without warning, he takes the exit on the left and smashes into the guard rail! Nothing can prepare you to stop immediately, let alone in a car on a wet road, driving 70 MPH. As soon as he hit the guard rail, the car spun to the right exposing the passenger side of the vehicle. I slammed on my brakes as hard as I could, but it was too late. I smashed into the side of the car at around 50-55 MPH, but luckily I hit the brace between the front and back seats. We totaled both cars in a matter of seconds, and now we're stuck. My friend is from the area, so after calling 911, he had friends come pick us up. This was turning out to be one of the worst weekends ever. I bought this car on a Tuesday, and three days later I have a busted lip, fractured wrist, and a smashed car. The drive back to base that Sunday was awkward since my friend's dad had to drive us back. The tension in the car was palpable.

Decisions

The claims process when you wreck a car is agonizing. There are a few people you have to call, paperwork to fill out, and tons of questions you are asked; it feels as if you're a criminal. After all that was over, the dealership called me and asked if I'd like to buy another car. Against my better judgement, I accepted the offer. I felt like I needed another car so I could go out with friends, on dates, to the store, anywhere I needed to go, plus I didn't have to walk. When it was all said and done, I bought a 1997 Chevy Lumina. This is the weakest engine, non-sporty, four door car. I knew not to mess around this time. I needed this car and was not trying to have two wrecked cars on my driving record at 19 years old. The car luckily lasted through five months of tech training, and two road trips.

I graduated tech training in July of 2002. My friends and I drove from Wichita Falls, Texas, to Tyndall AFB, Panama City, Florida, for another three weeks of training. The longest part of training is called "cold" training, where we sit in classrooms learning the aircraft systems and taking tests. Every so often, we'd go in the hangar and remove or install generators, hydraulic pumps, panels, or whatever we were learning at the time. We'd also perform inspections so the instructor could evaluate how we were progressing through the course. The second half of training is "hot" training, where we are on the flight line launching and recovering aircraft, and performing our duties that we will be entrusted with at our home station.

I was 19 years old, in Panama City Beach, FL, in the summer. My friends and I were always at the beach, always partying, and I was loving life. I would tell the girls I met that I was currently in the Air Force training program earning my pilot's wings. They ate it up, and I met a lot of girls who were mostly either on a family vacation or a girl's getaway weekend. This behavior began to be the norm and my decision to keep it up became easier and easier. Sometimes we get comfortable where we are. We act a certain way, we like how it makes us feel, and then somehow it becomes who we are. Negative and positive behaviors, skill sets, and habits can be reinforced over time. When we get away with something once, maybe twice, we start getting bolder, and start taking more and more risks. I firmly believe this philosophy began my slow downward spiral. I was enjoying going out with friends to the beach and hanging out on the strip meeting girls. Like the saying goes, "All good things come to an end."

I completed "hot" training and was on leave for a few weeks until it was time to go to my home station. In basic training, you get a list of bases that offer your job and you have to pick some stateside and overseas bases. I wrote in big letters "NO OVERSEAS" and I put a lot of stateside bases close to Michigan. I figured for the first few years, just in case this life wasn't for me, I wanted to be stationed close to home. Instead, I was sent to RAF Lakenheath, England, in September 2002. I was angry that I didn't get my first choice of base. I would have loved to stay in Florida, but I was stuck going to England.

At first I was bitter, never wanting to go anywhere or see anything, and was absolutely miserable for the first few weeks. You have two options when faced with this dilemma. You can be bitter and fester over what happened, or you can accept it and make the best of your surroundings. I had a lot of in-processing to complete and a dorm room to furnish. I received my enlistment bonus of $6000, and was ready to start spending! I bought a ton of clothes, TV, a Panasonic DVD surround sound system, DVDs, and a PlayStation 2 with games. The funny part is I still have that DVD system at the house; it still works, and is still plenty loud. I had a nice setup and was ready to endure this two year assignment. All I needed now was a car, and we all have seen the luck I have with those. The first car I bought was a 1986 Rover. The car was so old it even had a choke for cold weather starting. I kept thinking, "What is this thing, a lawnmower?" I didn't care since I had paid around $500-$600 for it. Going uphill in this manual transmission car was awful! I did eventually sell it, and bought a 1989 Skyline that I would drive for the duration of my time in England.

I had also found out the drinking age in England was 18 and Thursdays was karaoke night at the Enlisted Club. That's where all the enlisted personnel always hung out, and it became the place to unload at the end of a hard week. Everyone would go there to drink so I was always there drinking, and thus began my drinking journey. I can't remember a time that I either wasn't drinking or didn't have beer in the fridge and Jack Daniels on the counter. We had a lot of parties and cookouts in the dorms. It was so much fun that it reminded me of being back in Florida, or back home with the guys. If that got old, across the street from the base was a country bar called The Rod & Gun Club. This was the military hang out. It was within stumbling distance of the base and was such a great place to meet women and drink with friends. This became almost an every Friday and Saturday night event for the two years I was stationed in England. When we needed a break from The Rod, a group of us would venture out and see some of the bigger towns and cities. My absolute favorite place to hit the clubs was in Ipswich. The club was far enough away from the base where the girls loved Americans, and I could talk to as many girls as I wanted. This, again, became my normal behavior, and I enjoyed meeting girls and bringing them back to base.

Decisions

We'd all bring girls back from the club and continue drinking and partying back in the dorms. At one point it became almost a game to see who could pull more women from the clubs. This goes against everything I knew growing up, and against how I was raised. As I reflect back on the decisions I made so far, I can't help but think, somewhere, I have ruined a person's self-esteem or caused them some kind of pain.

While at work we would eat at the flightline kitchen, also known as the "Chow Hall." I was a broke airman spending all my money on weekend trips, bars, and alcohol, so much so, that I couldn't afford much food. I ate a lot at the chow halls since they were free because I lived in the dorms. At our flightline kitchen on my shift, there was this gorgeous blonde girl working there. I couldn't wait to go there every day so I could see her. Everyone would make fun of me when we would go inside because I would lock up in front of her; I didn't know what to say or do. I would always tell them, in my best Wayne's World voice, "She will be mine, oh yes, she will be mine." Every time I went to get food, I would get jittery, giggle, and turn beet red because I knew there was no way that beautiful girl was way out of my league. One day my suspicions were confirmed. I noticed she was wearing a wedding ring and my hopes of ever sparking interest between the two of us were crushed. The next few days didn't hold the same excitement as before because I knew I had no chance. At this point, all I could do was sit back and admire her beauty. I found out she frequented The Rod & Gun Club, and I finally worked up enough courage to talk to her. I found out that the hot chow hall chick and I actually had a lot in common. I would see her at the club and we'd dance and talk all night long. It took everything I had not to fall in love with her, but I couldn't help it. She

was so beautiful, funny, and we connected so quickly. I
knew I couldn't be with her, but it was nice to at least be
friends and talk to her when I could. In 2003, her time in
England was over and she PCS'd, which means Permanent
Change of Station, or being reassigned, to Mountain
Home, Idaho. In the spring of 2003, our unit was tasked to
deploy to the Middle East. I was ecstatic for this moment
because we went through all the training in basic, and we
were having exercises practicing our procedures in case
we deployed. Now it was time to put those skills to the
test and I was happy to be a part of it. We deployed to the
Middle East at a time of constant fighting and unrest. We
were flying around the clock, protecting the other services
that were fighting the ground war. We dropped a lot of
bombs those seven months, and although not as bad as I
heard it would be, it was still uneasy because at any point
we could be attacked. Back then, Americans were not the
most well liked people in the world. We were very busy
dropping bombs every day, fixing aircraft, out in the heat
for twelve hours, six days on and one day off work
schedule from June to December of 2003. During the
deployment, there was an opportunity to forward deploy
deeper onto front lines. I was single, with no attachments,
so of course, I volunteered to go. We were only there for
a few days fixing some broken jets, but that was enough
for me. I was really glad I joined the Air Force because the
Army and Marine Corps were constantly getting shot at
and bombed. For those few days when the sirens would
go off and we'd bunker down to get away from the
mortars and rockets coming in, I would get irritated and
kept thinking "enough already, we get it, you hate us."
The Army and Marines just shook it off because they were
used to it, but I only dealt with it for a couple days and was

quickly ready to leave. Those guys are the heroes, and the bravest guys I know.

A few months into the deployment, I was headed to the chow hall and I couldn't believe what I saw! The hot chow hall chick was on the same deployment as me, and her friend from England who PCS'd with her was there, too. Her unit deployed the same time we did. It was an amazing reunion and we couldn't believe we were deployed to the same location at the same time. I was so happy to see her and I finally had someone other than the guys at work to hang out with and talk to. It turns out, after leaving England her and her husband had a falling out and their marriage ended. Although I felt bad for her, I hoped in my heart I had another chance. I was so excited I could hardly contain myself and I think she knew it. We hung out almost every day, watching movies, talking about our past, where we were from, and where we wanted to be in the future. The deployment was so much better because of her and I was so thankful we spent it together. In England I was always chasing after women, and was mostly meaningless. The chow hall chick meant so much to me and we clicked and connected so well. When my deployment was over, it was hard to say goodbye, again. At least this time, we had a way to keep in touch.

My unit returned back to England in December of 2003 after 168 days in the desert. The chow hall chick and I would talk on the phone all the time through 2004. We were talking about maybe starting a relationship, or at least flying back and forth to visit with one another. I was falling so deeply in love with her; I was beginning to think she was the one. I was still going out and drinking, partying, meeting other girls, but the chow hall chick was still deployed and we weren't officially together. 2004 was the year that I was drinking every day after work, all weekend long, and that was all I did. I didn't have a lot of food in my dorm room, but I always made sure I had enough alcohol. I was told on more than one occasion that alcoholism runs in my family, but I didn't listen. When I came home to Michigan on leave, my cousin and I would always go out to the bar. We are as tight as brothers; we do everything together when I'm home. We both were alcoholics and drank all the time. My family would get extremely upset with us because we would get drunk and act stupid or do foolish things. I was 20 years old and on the verge of becoming a functioning alcoholic, but I didn't care. I stopped going to church back in tech school, I was meeting girls in bars and seeing how many I could sleep with every weekend, and drinking every day. I always said it would never happen to me. Well if you keep reading, you will find out that statement is hardly ever true in more than one way. I received orders and left England in September of 2004. I was ecstatic because I was being reassigned to Mountain Home, AFB, Idaho, the same place the chow hall chick was stationed. We decided to start a relationship and she became my girlfriend. We'd stay up all hours of the night just talking on the phone about everything, and about the future. I was now head over heels in love with her and I was so happy. Just one year prior I was afraid to talk to her in the flightline kitchen, and one year after that she's my girlfriend.

I have a problem with patience. The problem is I don't have any. I want what I want now, and strongly dislike waiting. When I decide in my heart to achieve a goal, I want to do it all that very instant, I don't like to wait. I also struggled with negativity and worry. I would constantly pull worry of the future into the present, and worry about every little thing. A relationship becomes unhealthy when someone is worried about everything all the time, especially when it's worrying about your significant leaving you for someone better. I know for a fact that I probably ruined the relationship, in a sense, because I was always worried that she'd find someone better, cheat on me, or not love me. I only had a few examples of what a healthy relationship looked like, and I was never told how to properly have a relationship with someone. All I saw growing up was fighting, yelling, and name calling in most of the relationships I witnessed. I knew I didn't want to be like that and so I fumbled my way through them all.

The chow hall chick met me at the airport when I arrived stateside at the end of my tour in England, and it felt amazing to hold her for the first time as my girlfriend. It felt like my life was finally making sense and I had a purpose; she was everything to me and I wanted to give her the world. We spent the night in Virginia and it felt amazing to finally talk all night in person since we had only talked on the phone the past eight months. We laid awake all night talking about our future plans, places we had been and where we still wanted to go, and everything in between. The best part of our relationship up to that point was the fact that it was not based on sex. We had hung out with each other during the deployment, and talked on the phone until we saw each other again. The love we had was deeply rooted and not based on false feelings. Those are the best relationships to have. When you can lay next to someone with neither of you expecting anything from the other person, but just to lay there with them, it makes all the difference.

In the morning, the chow hall chick and I got on a plane to Detroit to meet my family. Meeting the family has to be the most nerve racking moment in any couple's life. So many questions run through your mind. Most of the thoughts had to do with if my family would like her or accept her, but then I wondered if she would like them as well. I learned when getting to this stage that you're not only dating or in a relationship with that person, but the siblings and other family members are a packaged deal. It's even worse if one of you have kids. The whole time, I was hoping that my family wouldn't judge her or ask her too many questions because to me, this was the girl I wanted to marry. As usual, I worried for nothing. The chow hall chick and all my family had a great time and I was completely relieved. Everyone thought she was so sweet and she thought the same about my family, which brought us closer together.

After visiting, it was once again time to leave. Before leaving to England, I left my car at my mom's house. There are good days that bring you joy and memories, and then there are those bad days that bring you wisdom. Every experience and every situation is an opportunity to learn something, and to be better than you were yesterday. My younger sister was allowed to drive my car while I was away. She was a new driver and my mother let her drive my Chevy Lumina I left for her to take care of. When I saw the state of the car, I felt betrayed. There were dents and dings all over the car, and the rear taillight was busted out from my sister backing into someone. I did not expect to come home and have to fix my damaged car before departing on a cross country drive from Michigan to Idaho. I got the car fixed and left Michigan for the next part of my journey.

When the chow hall chick and I got to Idaho, that's when I found out that she would be leaving to go to Full Sail University in Winter Park, FL. I was under the impression that we would live together, but she had other plans and decided not to re-enlist in the Air Force. I got to

Decisions

spend a week or so with her before we drove from Idaho to Florida. She already had an apartment, school setup, and so she began a new chapter of her life. This was a bitter pill for me to swallow. I felt betrayed and hurt, but also happy for her new journey. I wanted to be with her so badly, and I felt like I didn't matter because she would have rather moved away than stay with me. The hurt I felt, and the grudge I carried, would eventually put a huge strain on our relationship. I suppose I underestimated her feelings and didn't really ask her how she felt about everything. She would always tell me she loved me, but I also wasn't being very supportive for her wanting to go to school. In these moments, you have to make clear what is on your mind and in your heart, yet say it in a way that is respectful for the relationship. I dropped her off in Florida and I didn't leave on the best of terms. I made her feel guilty for choosing this path rather than staying and living with me until my current enlistment was complete.

For the next five months, my emotions were like a downward spiral. I was speeding down a dark road that led to nowhere. I was drinking heavier now and would cry myself to sleep every couple weeks. I was wallowing in self-pity instead of enjoying life and being grateful that I had someone special no matter how far away. When the chow hall chick left, I stayed in her old room in the apartment she shared with her best friend from England. Although we became friends, it was very hard for her to see me mope around while also trying to be a loyal friend to the chow hall chick. I know now I was a terrible roommate and I put her in a very uncomfortable situation. I focused so hard on the negatives of everything around me that I didn't appreciate or show gratitude where I should have. Relationships were strained, co-workers couldn't count on me, and my performance at work was suffering. It would not end there.

During spring break 2005, the chow hall chick and I had plans for her to come to Idaho to visit. Instead, what I got was a phone call from her to tell me she wasn't coming. In addition, she had spent the last week in Daytona, FL, at Bike Week, and cheated on me. That is the worst feeling for anyone, knowing someone you love betrayed you. It wasn't just at Bike Week, she was having a relationship with someone else where she lived and didn't need me anymore. She said that she felt bad, but couldn't handle the long distance between us and needed to move on, since it was becoming a problem for her to concentrate on school. I felt like the lowest form of life at that point. In that moment, life seemed hopeless. I was hitting rock bottom fast and I had nowhere to turn. I chose to go to Idaho because that's where the chow hall chick was, but then she left. I didn't like where I worked, I had very few friends since all I ever did was come home, drink, and mope around the apartment. This became very personal for me and I hated what I had become. Instead of changing, I chose to blame others for how my life was going. The best decision to make is to acknowledge and accept adversity and grow from it. This was not in my nature at the time and everyone around me suffered because of my actions. This is a lot to bear on someone when all you tell yourself is that everything is your fault and you never do anything right. Repetitive behavior, positive or negative, becomes easier and easier the more it happens, and is then reinforced. Humans are creatures of habit and we constantly fall into cognitive traps that drag us down. I was in the All-or-Nothing stage; always, never, everything. I always messed things up, thought "I'm never going to be happy", and everything is horrible.

Decisions

My drinking had become an everyday an every night habit, and I was medicating myself to feel numb. There are three common ways people deal with pain, or adversity: 1) They ignore it and hope it goes away, 2) They medicate it with either drugs or alcohol to feel numb to the pain, which in my case was alcohol, or 3) They acknowledge it and take immediate steps to form an action plan to rise above. This is what's called your Fight-or-Flight instincts. Do you run away from all your problems? Are you a fighter, fighting every battle put in front of you? I used to do both. I would fight every battle at work, but wouldn't deal with my personal issues. By acting in this way, what I had created was a melting pot or powder keg that eventually was ready to explode. I was no longer drinking just to numb the pain of losing the hot chow hall chick, but to escape a place I didn't want to work at. I would fight every battle at work because I didn't enjoy being there, and since I was hurting, I made everyone else suffer with me. Coupled with my roommate, the chow hall chick's friend, now receiving a new assignment and moving, I was left to my own vices.

My drinking nearly cost me my career when I woke up late for work one morning. I didn't just wake up late; I woke up two hours after I was supposed to report for duty, and I reeked of alcohol. As soon as I got to work, I reported to my Flight Chief. I was asked why I was late to work and my response was, "Because I had been drinking all night because I'm dealing with a lot right now." This response caused a chain reaction and I was sent to the Mental Health Clinic on base. I was read my rights, interviewed, had blood drawn, and given paperwork to sign. About an hour later, my BAC (Blood Alcohol Content) came back 0.08. It was estimated by the authorities that when I drove to work, my BAC was 0.12. I was told that

Decisions

0.02 BAC leaves your body approximately every hour, and since it had been two to three hours since I drove, I was allegedly over the legal limit and drunk coming into work. I was administered an Article 112 for violation of the Uniform Code of Military Justice. The Article 112 is Drunk on Duty, and comes with a lot of punishment to follow. I was reprimanded and sent to ADAPT, which is Alcohol and Drug Prevention and Treatment, for two weeks. I was aware that I had become a problem, but I didn't know how to fix it. I was hurting so bad, I hated my work center, and I felt like I had no purpose. The year prior to this, I lost my Aunt Hope, who I would talk to about relationships and obstacles in my life. Now who do I turn to? I was ordered NOT to consume alcohol at any time during this two week long program. I was to show up on time with a positive attitude, and any violation of the many other rules would result in harsher punishment, even discharge. I didn't drink for the first few days, but since they weren't blood testing anyone, I figured I'd drink in moderation. I finished up the program and went back to drinking. I don't know why I didn't take the program more seriously, maybe because of everything I was dealing with, I didn't value my career as much as I used to. I didn't value life very much and my decisions were reckless. These decisions I made forced my leadership to send me to Security Forces Augmentee Duty. For the next four months, I worked right alongside Security Forces, which is the Air Force's Military Police. If I messed up in any way, I would be kicked out of the Air Force. I finished my treatment, but the pain was still there. Not only was I a failure at relationships, I felt like I let my co-workers down. When I returned to work, it was hard to look people in the face because it felt like I was being judged. Eventually, personnel came and went, and we moved on. I, however, continued to drink.

Decisions

Sometimes we have to live the same lesson over and over again until we learn from it. The decisions we make will never only impact ourselves. My decisions were impacting my co-workers, the military mission, and drinking and driving could have impacted innocent families if there was a car accident. My decisions were beginning to leave a trail of wreckage behind me.

I had a few other relationships after the hot chow hall chick, but I was in no way healed or ready to move on. I was always chasing after something to bring me the joy I had felt when we were together, but all I had done was fill myself with more emptiness. No matter what I did or who I was with, nothing made me happy. I decided one day that I needed a change of scenery, so I moved out of the apartment to a friend's house in Boise. This may not have been the best decision, considering that I was now sleeping on his couch and rooming with him and his girlfriend. This was only temporary since his lease was up and he was moving into a place for him and his girlfriend. I had nowhere to live, and after a few nights of sleeping in my car, another friend let me live with him. Again, I'm sleeping on a friend's couch just to have a place to sleep, all the while, drinking and not performing like I should at work. My performance and relationships were not on a healthy level and I surrounded myself with everyone else's hurt and pain so I wouldn't feel alone. Some say you're defined by the company you keep. I believe there is some truth to that statement but it boils down to perspective. I didn't see any blessings in my life, just pain and misery. I was sleeping on people's couches and barely getting by in life. This was not how I imagined my life going and I certainly wasn't praying to God for help. At this point in my life, I was cursing Him for everything wrong in my life, but not looking at the decisions I made up to this point that got me in the situation I was in. You can't fix what's going on around you until you fix what's going on inside you.

Speaking of stupid decisions, my friends and I raced a lot. The Chevy Lumina ended up blowing a motor when I let someone borrow it. I didn't care because I was driving a 1992 Mustang LX and the Chevy was like a spare car since the mustang was built for racing and was a gas hog. When the Mustang engine started burning oil, I figured instead of fixing it, I'd sell the car, and buy something else. I sold the Mustang and bought a 2000 VW Jetta VR6. This car had leather and heated seats, sunroof, and bright red paint. I put so much money into this car, buying rims and tires, intake, exhaust, and a GIAC chip. I loved this car and raced it every chance I got. This was my autocross car and I became extremely skilled. One snowy day we all got the bright idea to drift our cars in a parking lot full of fresh snow. For the time being, I felt happy. When you're in a down season of your life, you don't make the best decisions. You tend to go with the flow rather than being the thermostat that changes the dynamic of the situation. I was going with the flow and doing what everyone else was doing. I was drifting in a newly snow filled parking lot and slid into the curb, breaking my rear axle. What have I done? My decision making skills were not the best in the world and I knew this was going to be an expensive mistake. The bill was $900, and since I couldn't pay for it, I opened a credit account with the mechanic shop, Les Schwab. It was at this very moment I discovered CREDIT. Now, I could charge whatever I want and pay it back later. Again, my decision making skills are lacking because I have an "I don't care" attitude about everything. It turns out credit hurts just like everything else.

Decisions

While the Jetta was in the shop, I rented a car. So far, I had had very little luck keeping cars, or even having decent vehicles that don't have some kind of major issue. The rental car lasted about two weeks until I was caught drifting in another parking lot and AGAIN slid into a curb. This time, I broke the front tie rods and had to get them fixed. I took it to the shop to get fixed, but they confiscated the car and I was stuck walking. I found myself at a dealership in front of a 90's Ford Probe. I used my last $1800 to buy this car so I would have some mode of transportation. I drove the Ford Probe until my Jetta was fixed. I sold the probe to a friend to help pay some of my bills, since all the credit bills were now just about due. I had to learn from my mistakes at some point, so I figured now was a good time to start. I think I fell short...

I moved out of my friend's house, off his couch, and rented a house with two other roommates in late 2005. This would have been a great start, but, we were having parties every weekend and my drinking had gotten just as bad as before. Four months later, I received a call from my Flight Chief telling me to come to work now because I had a set of orders re-assigning me to Hill AFB, Utah. I had 30 days to out process my unit, pack up my house, and move to Utah. I was looking forward to going somewhere else. The year and a half that I spent in Idaho, was filled with some of the worst moments of my life. I lost the chow hall chick, couldn't handle other relationships, wrecked two cars, slept in my car, slept on friends' couches, and was almost kicked out of the Air Force. I welcomed this change and I was ready to move on! Sometimes our lives have to be completely shaken up, changed, and rearranged to relocate us to the place we're meant to be. I can look back on my life and pinpoint every time God's grace was shown. I was stuck in a dark place

Decisions

with nowhere to turn until I received orders to move away. Finally, there was a light at the end of a long, dark hole.

I was re-assigned to Utah in April of 2006. My friend from Idaho came with me to get away from Boise, and we moved into a two bedroom apartment together. My apartment building had a smoke pit in the middle of a court yard, and that's where I met Candi. Her apartment building was right next to mine, yet she hung out at my building with her friends. It was nice because I thought she was so beautiful, and I got to see her just about every day. I asked her out but she could see right through my cheesy pickup lines and hidden agenda. For months I would talk to her, and tell her how great of a guy I was just to get close enough to sleep with her. In the end, in every relationship except with the chow hall chick, that was always my goal. I would go to the bars to meet girls and try to pick up women everywhere I went just to have sex with them. That was my end game until I met the chow hall chick. She was the one I wanted to be with, but it was obvious she didn't feel the same, so here I was chasing after love the wrong way. Candi was not having any of it. She could see right through what I was trying to do. I wanted to get with her so bad that I even met her mom and told her how wonderful I was, and how great I would treat Candi if we were together. I talked to her family and friends, I put on this whole show to make myself look good, and I even made them dinner. All the while, I was still drinking and partying with my own hidden agendas.

Candi is Puerto Rican, about 4' 10", so hot with a beautiful smile, and a hell of a spark plug for a personality and attitude. She grew up rough like I did, divorced parents, unstable living conditions, and poor examples all around her. As I talked to her more, I saw that we had a

Decisions

few things in common. I wasn't so focused on my own agenda as much. I enjoyed talking to Candi late at night at the smoke table, unloading the day's problems on one another, and just making small talk. I knew no matter how much crap I dealt with that day, if Candi was smoking she'd listen to me and make me feel better.

"Idaho Boy" was living with me and he would hang out with us as well. There would be four or five of us sitting at the picnic table smoking, talking about our day, the area, what was new in the world, and it was a great time. Idaho Boy liked Candi, but she didn't want him either. He and I would go back and forth over who was going to sleep with and/or date what girl. Eventually, since Candi said she didn't want me, I decided to make her jealous by sleeping with one of her friends in our group. This friend of hers was always out there smoking, so I figured, "What the heck, Candi doesn't want me." My track record for decision making was batting 1000, and this would be no different. My decision to sleep with Candi's friend caused a huge issue once she found out, and even the other girls that would smoke with us thought I was a bad person for doing that. Looking back now, I realize it was not the best route to take in order to grab Candi's attention, and was also extremely immature. That's how I was back then, immature and didn't care about anyone else's feelings. I wanted what I wanted and I thought I was more important than everyone else. I had no regard for anyone else's feelings or opinions, and was severely closed minded and closed off. I learned how to hide a lot of pain I was dealing with from the breakup with the chow hall chick, the loss of my aunt, new job, new place, and the uncertainty of the future. Again, I was pulling worry from the future into today, only this time it was accompanied by yesterday's pain. This mentality is

Decisions

very unhealthy and causes hopelessness to take over your life. We start to lie to ourselves about how we feel, justify why or how we react to certain situations, and eventually stress ourselves out until we break. One thing I've learned is that God must break us in order to remake us.

Idaho Boy and I lived in the apartment complex for six months until the lease was up. We packed up and rented a three bedroom house with a finished basement, where he slept. We would have parties almost every weekend. We didn't have a lot of food but we always made sure we had enough beer, because this was my priority and a hard habit to break. I lived off Ramen Noodles, pizza rolls, and take out. I was single and had no responsibility other than to wake up, go to work, pay bills, come home and drink. I didn't really care too much about anything, plus, Boise, Idaho was only a short four hour drive away, so I spent a few weekends driving back and forth to see old friends. I would eventually lose contact with Candi and everyone else I met while living at the apartments.

I decided one day I needed an extra job. I was already a DJ at the enlisted club, which is our bar on Hill AFB, on the weekends. I still needed more money for things I wanted. I was racking up debt quickly, paying a lot of money towards alcohol, partying, and eating out. I got another job during the week at Discount Tire. I would work there in the mornings, and then leave around 2 P.M. to be at the military job by 3 P.M. I started wearing myself out because on the weekends I was a DJ, and I didn't get much time to sleep in. I did enjoy the amount of money I was making, but had I made better financial decisions, I wouldn't have been in the situation I was in. Two of the hardest things in life to be disciplined about are budgeting and spending. Most people say you need to save money so that you have it, and you need to build wealth. My thought was, "Well, you can't take it with you when you die." I wasn't concerned with building up my children's future since I didn't have any kids, that I was aware of. Instead, I blew my money away on hundred dollar bar tabs, trips and vacations, and just stuff to fill the emptiness in my life. I realize now that this behavior is unhealthy for everyone around me and it caused some heavy conflict.

While working at Discount Tire, I met a great friend, who could do the best Arnold Schwarzenegger impressions. "Little Arnold" was just like me, as he was always drinking, working on cars, and lived a care free life. He was living with his mom and I asked him to move in with me and Idaho Boy, since he was spending a lot of time over at our house anyway. He moved into the room upstairs next to mine. It was awesome having him there because we partied all the time, all weekend long, and we became very close friends. We did everything together, and for the first time, I was really enjoying my life. I still didn't have a stable female relationship, but I was working on it.

I met a Mormon girl that I thought would have helped me settle down. I felt ready to open myself back up, that it was time to let go of the chow hall chick, and stop dwelling on my past hurts. I was actually willing to stop smoking because of her. She had an infant from a previous relationship, but I didn't care. She was cute and I wanted to see where it would go. We hung out a few times and I could tell she was real timid around me. As soon as I'd get close to her, she would move away like she didn't want to be held or cuddled. I'm not sure what happened, but I was positive the past relationship messed up her view of any future relationships which led to trust issues. I met her parents and tried to be the nice young man and put on a show so they'd think I was a decent guy. I doubt that went over smoothly considering I got a phone call a few days later from her, telling me she couldn't see me anymore because I wasn't Mormon. My beliefs and thoughts were, "Here we go again." Every time I tried to put myself out there for someone I got rejected or it just wouldn't work out. I was getting so sick and tired of feeling this way. After a while, having meaningless sex got boring and I eventually wanted to find someone that could give it meaning. I was once again feeling depressed, feeling like no one wanted me and no one loved me. My negative thinking and my catastrophizing were beginning to show and I just wanted to get away from it. This was the first time I seriously contemplated suicide. I had thought about it before when the hot chow hall chick ripped my heart out of my chest and threw it away, figuratively speaking. The pain from not having fully dealt with the way the chow hall chick and I ended was creeping back into my life. I compared every relationship to what the chow hall chick and I had and it was apparent that not only was I not healed, but I had not accepted the feelings that I was harboring and all my relationships suffered. You can't change what's going on around you, until you change what's going on inside you.

I went to Boise, Idaho, to go visit some friends since my feelings were at an all-time low. I met up with some old friends and a girl I had seen before but never got a chance to talk to. She and I finally connected and I felt a new sense of hope. She was also blonde like the hot chow hall chick; seems to be a pattern to all my relationships thus far. I was trying to find a replacement or find someone that resembled the chow hall chick, but all I was doing was living in the past. It's very difficult to move on with your life if you're not ready. At some point, you have to move forward and let go of your hurt. If you don't, it will consume your every thought and every part of your everyday life. For some reason we hold on to the pain, the memories, and the moments in the past whether they are good or bad. Somehow we feel like if we let them go, we don't care about the past or it didn't mean anything to us. Every day is an opportunity to write another page into our story book of life. Turn the page; there's no sense in rereading yesterday's news. Two years after breaking up with the chow hall chick, I was still feeling the effects of not accepting what had happened. I was talking to girls who reminded me of her, who had the same features as her, or acted and talked like her. I talked to one more girl who fit the bill, and invited her to a party at my house in Utah.

A few weeks later, after talking with the new girl on the phone, she and some friends were finally going to come to my house to visit. The date was St. Patrick's Day. Idaho Boy, Little Arnold, and I went all out putting together a huge party. There were definitely over a hundred people that came to drink and have a good time. My house had the reputation of being the "party house." I was very naïve to think that every single person at my house was a friend, but you don't find out who your true friends are until tragedy strikes. I'd much rather have friends that have my back behind my back, than be associated with people who *say* they have your back, but run at the first sign of trouble.

At approximately 2 A.M. St. Patrick's Day 2007, Idaho Boy and I were cleaning up the kitchen of beer bottles, spilt beer, food, and all the trash. Little Arnold came bursting through the front door yelling that the house was on fire! I told him to stop playing around, but just then there was a loud explosion from the garage area.

Decisions

I ran to the door that connected the house to the garage and the whole side of the house and garage were on fire! The flames were so intense, we couldn't stay out there too long because the heat was burning our faces. I tried everything to put it out, but the flames were too much. The fire had engulfed the garage and the two front bedrooms, one of which was Little Arnold's. We called 911 and I told everyone to leave. I ran upstairs as fast as I could to grab my puppies that were in their cage in my room, my laptop, and my military uniforms. I was in and out of the house in a matter of seconds. Idaho Boy, Little Arnold, and I all watched our house burn, until Little Arnold asked if that girl had made it out. I completely forgot that the girl from Idaho was asleep in my bed! She had drank too much earlier and I told her to go lay down. Now, the house is on fire and I have no idea if she's dead or alive. I panicked and ran over to alert the fire department that she still may be inside the house. Like a bad scene out of a movie, they brought her out, soot and smoked stained clothes and all, with the fireman's coat and a gas mask on her. I felt really bad, but then I remembered we were supposed to hook up that night and felt disappointed that I missed out on that. I had always cared more about my needs than anyone else and it almost cost someone their life!

The fire was extinguished about an hour or so later. The upstairs was just a shell of what it used to be. Little Arnold lost almost every single thing he owned, and all my stuff was, at a minimum, smoke damaged. I slept in the bedroom in the back of the house, next to Little Arnold's room. The fire didn't quite reach all the way into my room, but the ceiling was burned and my room was pretty close to being burned up. My life literally just went up in flames. I was too busy trying to impress everyone else, trying to be the party guy, trying to be liked by everyone, that I let things get way out of control and I lost everything. It turned out, since I was renting, the home owner had an arson investigator come out and sure enough, someone deliberately set our house on fire. Investigators arrested some kid and his uncle who set fires around our neighborhood. Not only was our house set on fire, a car we were working on in our garage was set fire to and even had a rag on fire in the gas tank filler neck. Luckily, we emptied the gas tank so we were safe, but still scary that someone would go this far. I didn't have much to move since everything was either burned or smoke damaged. On the way out my thought was "I guess I don't get the deposit back on this house...."

Red Cross helped me get into a hotel room for three days, and USAA gave me $1000. The worst part about it was I had to put my two pit bulls into a shelter since I couldn't have them in the hotel room. Idaho Boy decided that he'd had enough and left to go back to Boise, Idaho. Little Arnold moved back in with his mom. Out of everyone that came over that night and that I thought were my friends, only Little Arnold was left to deal with the aftermath with me, or so I thought. Out of the blue, Candi, the girl I tried to hook up with back at the apartments, was calling to check on me. She wanted nothing to do with me before and I couldn't believe she cared enough to call me. Not one of the people who attended our party called to check and see how we were doing; not one person called to see if they could help us or if we even needed help. I never heard from any of them again. When Candi called, it was a huge surprise. She offered to help me with anything I needed, and even offered me a place to stay. I thanked her, and she helped me gather what was left of my belongings and I moved into her apartment. I was right back where I started. I was so excited to be living somewhere I could have my dogs that we rushed over to the shelter to pick them up. Nothing could prepare me for what happened next. One of my pit bulls, the male, bit one of the animal control officers and they decided to put him down. No one called me; no one said a word for two days, the shelter made the decision on their own to euthanize my dog. I was crushed that they would do something like that. After everything I just went through, I did not need to add a dead dog to my list. I took my female pit bull and left, crying and broken.

"Lessons in life will be repeated until they are learned."
– Frank Sonnenberg, Author/America's Top 100 Thought Leader -

"The World ain't all sunshine and rainbows. It's a very mean and nasty place, and I don't care how tough you are, it will be beat you to your knees and keep you there permanently if you let it. You, me, or nobody is gonna hit as hard as life. But it ain't about how hard ya hit. It's about how hard you can get hit and keep moving forward. How much you can take and keep moving forward. That's how winning is done!
– Sylvester Stallone, Rocky Balboa Movie –

"The Lord is my light and my salvation – whom shall I fear? The Lord is the stronghold of my life – of whom shall I be afraid? When the wicked advance against me to devour me, it is my enemies and my foes who will stumble and fall. Though an army besiege me, my heart will not fear; though war break out against me, even then I will be confident."
– Psalm 27:1-3 –

BROKEN & BRUISED

5

Do you live with regret? Have you experienced something so horrible that it stays with you, even today? Our behavior is directly related to past experiences, culture, decisions, values, and our family. It is in these aspects that we base a lot of our decisions. We saw our grandparents, parents, aunts and uncles make decisions both good and bad. The only parenting examples I had were my mom who was now divorced twice, my dad who I spent every other weekend with for most of my life, and aunts and uncles I spent little time with. Up to this point, I had very few examples I could pull from as to what real love in relationships looked and felt like, how to communicate, and become a productive relationship partner. I had lost those who I thought were my friends, lost my house in a fire, my belongings, one of my dogs, and once again my coworkers view me as untrustworthy. I'm feeling broken, depressed, fighting to stay afloat. It's very lonely when you're a self-destructive person; relationships are ruined and you have no one left to rely on. I was on the verge of giving up after everything I had just gone through, but out of nowhere, an unexpected saving grace.

Decisions

I moved in with Candi towards the end of March, after finally closing the chapter on the house fire. At first, I was sleeping on the couch. Her mom was staying in the spare bedroom with Anastasia, who was four months old. This living arrangement was much different than what I was used to. Gaven, her son who was three years old at the time, visited every two weeks per the verbal parenting agreement between Candi and her ex. I wasn't used to having kids around, or living with a mom. I was definitely the outsider and didn't know how long this would last. Pretty soon, instead of sleeping on the couch, I was sleeping in Candi's room, and we decided to make it official. We were together from April to July of 2007 when I asked Candi to marry me. I know it was only a short time we had actually been together, but we had known each other since April 2006. We hung out, talked, and were friends that whole time until we lost touch. It seemed like the responsible thing to do. She was single with two kids, and I thought since we were falling in love and I was finally happy, that this would have been the best course of action. We were married at a courthouse on July 27th, 2007. We didn't have money for a honeymoon, and we only had immediate family as part of the courthouse ceremony. Not exactly how I planned my wedding, but I made it work. We moved out of the apartment and into our first house. We were renting and we began to live like a family. The only difference was, I wasn't exactly ready to give up my partying lifestyle. I still wanted to drink, play video games, and hang out with friends. I always thought that a marriage was just a ring and a piece of paper. Why did I need to stop being who I was and stop what I was doing? I learned later on that marriage is so much more. I didn't want to give up my "single life" behaviors I was living, mainly because the marriage didn't feel personal. I wasn't ready to fully commit to marriage, the rules, and the "tied down" life. I loved Candi, but she didn't make it easy either. I felt as though I was always getting yelled at for something. We started to argue, fight about everything, and I felt like our relationship had changed drastically from the moment we got married. Before then, we didn't argue at all and we talked to each other with love and respect, and we dealt with problems head on. Now, we just yelled at each other, treated each other badly, and didn't deal with issues well. This was not what I signed up for and I wanted out, fast!

As soon as we were married, Candi's ex, Gaven's biological father, wouldn't return Gaven to Candi after his visitation time. They both agreed on a two week period of visitation. He felt like he was being replaced, and therefore was unwilling to let Gaven live with us. Since they only had a "verbal" agreement, the authorities were unable to do anything, and we had to hire a lawyer and go to court. This has to be the most drawn out, ludacris, horrible experience anyone has to go through. It was over a month until we could get a court date. Meanwhile, Gaven was still with his father and Candi was unable to see him. Lawyers are expensive, and the court system is cluttered with court cases, appeals, and drawn out processes. Almost two months later, we finally had a legal binding agreement for a two week visitation period. It was also stated, Gaven could not be withheld from either parent, and must be split visitation equally. This was such a relief. Candi was so worried about Gaven being kidnapped again; she finally had the legal contract to prevent it. I couldn't believe as an adult that I'm dealing with the same issues I dealt with as a kid. I swore I would never let my kids go through what I went through, but sometimes, everything happens for a reason.

Decisions

My job in the Air Force while stationed at Hill AFB was an Aircraft Battle Damage Repair Technician. My sole purpose was to be sent out as part of a Depot Field Team to fix aircraft too severely damaged to be repaired by home station personnel. From 2006 to 2009, I was on the road a lot. I was home for a few a months, gone for a week, home for a week, gone for two months, home for a few days, then back out for a month. In 2008 alone, I was on the road a total of 200+ non-consecutive days. This coming and going added more stress on an already unstable and fractured marriage. She wanted to talk to me on the phone all day every day and she was still adjusting to military life. I was on the road working and traveling. She hated me being gone all the time, especially when she would call and our team was headed out to the bar. When you're TDY, or temporary assignment, we work hard and play hard. I traveled overseas, Michigan, Las Vegas, Florida, Arizona, and many other locations, and I rocked them all! I loved being on the road and experiencing all the different cultures and party spots that the city we were in had to offer. Candi was not impressed and I think she felt like I wasn't taking our marriage seriously. Our team was always at the bar, which I think worried her since she knew my family history of alcoholism. I was very selfish, and didn't respect the fact that Candi was more worried about me rather than trying to control me.

It was very hard coming back home from being on the road. There was one instance where I came home from Florida after a three week trip, and turned around three days later and returned to Florida for another two weeks. I loved going to Florida. Not the beaches or the sharks, but the clubs are amazing in Panama City. A lot of my friends I was close to while stationed in England were stationed in Florida and we reconnected and picked up right where we left off. Candi was not happy and there were times we would fight over the phone about me going out. I always felt like she was trying to control me and stop me from having fun, like she was jealous in some way. I was hanging out with other married guys whose wives never acted like she would. The difference was, their husbands weren't alcoholics and never needed help leaving a bar. There were a few times I was overly intoxicated and was carried out of the bar and thrown into the back seat of the car. I'm not proud of it and quite embarrassed now about my behavior. I was very selfish and didn't have a care in the world. After all that, coming home can be hard. You have to settle down, reconnect with family, and try to be what you need to be, all he while knowing you will leave again. That lifestyle puts a strain on relationships and really tests the strength of your bond.

Candi and I had been married a year. I had been away so much and she felt like this wasn't what she signed up for. I started hanging out with Little Arnold again, a lot. We were drinking, watching UFC PPVs, and having fun, but Candi was unimpressed. I think she had good intentions but did not communicate them well. It seemed like she was being more of a mother than she was my wife and we started to resent each other. All the built up resentment and anger we had resulted in a huge fight and everything in our life exploded. We held on to so much anger and held in so many issues that we both erupted and screamed at each other for how awful we were as a married couple and how unhappy we made each other. I remember telling her I was done with our marriage and I didn't want her anymore. I sat down in the living room to gather my thoughts and out of nowhere there was pounding at the front door. Four city police officers were at my door with agitated expressions and hands on their weapons. I was pulled outside and searched. It was reported that Candi and I were fighting and that I had a gun. As this is a true statement, the fact is, the gun is always locked away in the closet. I do have a gun, but it just was not on me personally. The officers were told that I had a gun, which in their minds meant I had a gun pointed at my wife's face and wanted to do bodily harm. When they didn't find any weapons on me, I was escorted back inside and placed on the couch. An officer stood next to me while the other three questioned Candi. I could hear her yelling about how I was a horrible husband; I cheat, lie, am an alcoholic who refuses help, and a piece of crap. When they couldn't calm her down, the officers then came to question me. I was literally reliving my childhood in this moment. I swore I would never turn out like my ex-stepdad, but here I was being interrogated on the night's events. I calmly told them what we had been fighting about and the series of events leading up to the blowout. As I was explaining it all to the police, everyone in the room could hear Candi yelling down the stairs from the bedroom that I was lying and that I was a piece of crap. The police kept telling her to stay calm, but she wouldn't. She yelled again and again as I explained our lifestyle and our relationship. The police had had enough and told her to pack some bags for her and the kids because it was clear she wasn't going to stay calm after they left and it was time to go. They made her leave, and the one officer that stood with me this whole time leans in and says to me, "Son, you need to get away from this craziness." I chuckled and said "I know", and closed the door behind the police.

I was left in complete silence. I was reliving my childhood all over again, except no one was beaten or thrown into walls or furniture. I sat on the couch trying to sort out the events that had just transpired, and how I got to this point. I felt this weight on my body and couldn't move. I sat there, puzzled, confused, sad, mad, and I couldn't handle the flood of emotions that rushed through my body like a tidal wave. I went into the kitchen to get the Jack Daniels and I drank the rest of my night away. It was all I knew how to do. I would crawl into a bottle and try to mask my feelings from the world. The only result is that you think about it harder, and you feel these feelings stronger, because after all, alcohol is a depressant, contrary to popular belief. This makes you want to drink more so you can run away faster, but the result is you eventually pass out, yet the problem still remains.

The next few days were hectic. Candi's family was harassing me and telling me how I was no good. Candi came home and our relationship was worse. We fought harder, louder, and the dynamic became emotional for everyone. My co-workers could tell that I had an inner battle going on inside me, but they never knew what it was. My Flight Chief and my immediate supervisor pulled me into the office and grilled me about how I was doing, what was keeping my attitude down, why was I not motivated...I was getting interrogated like I committed a crime. When you know someone, you know. They knew there was no way I would come out with what I was feeling freely, especially since I was an emotionally closed off guy to begin with. I didn't tell people how I felt, I didn't let anyone in, and surely didn't talk about my feelings or show off my wounds for the world to see. I was asked repeatedly if there was anything I'd like to say, what was going on, what was it that I was holding back, what was it that I was carrying around with me that I wouldn't let anyone else see. I finally gave in and spelled it all out. My supervisor was shaking his head in disbelief of what I'd had to deal with over that past year. My house burned down, my dog was killed, everyone who I thought were friends of mine left, I was a functioning alcoholic, in debt, and then I was married with two kids with which, one of them had a crazy father who made our lives difficult and the most current was the possibility of divorce. I felt like I had the year from hell and I wasn't sure how to handle it all. My childhood was haunting me and I didn't want anyone to have to go through what I went through. I listened to what my bosses had to say and I left the office with a little bit of a boost. When I got home, it was a different story.

I was outside in the front yard doing yard work when Candi's mom and step-dad stopped by. They were yelling at me about how horrible of a person I was and threatening me if I ever hurt their daughter. I called my supervisor to inform him of what had happened, and I was told to pack some clothes and stay at his house. Candi was furious that I was leaving instead of staying to discuss our issues. She said I was running away from all my problems, but I wanted to get out of there fast in case more of her family came over. We had young kids and I did not want them to see any of the problems or altercations. Candi stood right in front of the door blocking me from leaving. I knew I couldn't touch her because it may have been considered domestic battery or assault, and I was not willing to add that to the list of problems. I called my supervisor again and he said he was coming over with the police. When they arrived, we were yelling at each other and fighting about me leaving and every other problem we'd ever had. The police and my supervisor split us up and after giving my version of the story, we left. I stayed at his house for a few days until I could schedule an appointment with the courts to file an order of protection. I wanted her and her family gone. I was paying the rent and all the bills and since she was from Utah, I saw no reason for me to leave when I had no other place to go. My petition was filed and she was forced to vacate our house with the understanding she was not to come around me, the house, my job, and it extended to her family as well. I finally felt at peace, but there was some guilt as well. I was in a room before the hearing with nothing but battered women who were scared for their lives, who wanted to get away from the torture and pain that was being done to them. Here I was wanting to be left alone, but these women feared for their lives. I felt as though I was acting like a baby, like I couldn't handle this on my own. Men aren't supposed to get protective orders against their wives and their family, men are supposed to fight and be strong. I felt like a sissy and guilty for what I thought was the easy out. The scars I had weren't physical but emotional from the yelling, screaming, verbal altercations, mean nasty remarks we would say to each other, and the occasional dodging of a remote control or a drinking glass that was thrown at my head. Compared to these women, or my mother, I had it good. I was sick to my stomach when I got home to the empty house and seeing her clothes gone. Now, it became real.

Keeping your mind occupied on everything BUT your problems can prove to be a daunting task. I tried everything to stay away from home, not drink, or think too deeply about what was happening. I missed Candi and the kids, but I know we did not have a healthy relationship. My whole life I was told never to stay in an unhealthy relationship, emotionally or physically, for the sake of the children. That's very difficult when you love them, and worry about their safety. All I thought about was how those kids were holding up through all of this. Did they understand? Was Candi and her family filling their heads with lies about me supposedly being a horrible person? Does anyone miss me? I started blaming myself for breaking up our family. I started wondering if there was anything else I could have done to fix our marriage. More and more thoughts started creeping into my mind that changed my perspective of the situation. When you're alone, you have a lot of time to think. Add that on top of someone who is still drinking heavily going through a major adversity, nothing positive comes from it. Also add the fact that it's Christmas time and there's no decorations, no presents, no children laughing, no children in their beds dreaming of what Santa Claus is going to bring them. Christmas has always been my most favorite time of the year! Our house looks like a Christmas cloud parked over us and threw up. Our house could be compared to the Griswold's house in the movie National Lampoon's Christmas Vacation. We had lights and decorations inside and out, as bright as could be, and people would drive by our house to get pictures and take selfies, it was amazing! Now, it was replaced with darkness. Christmas 2008 will forever be the worst Christmas of my life.

I talked to my family Christmas Eve night. The tradition of gathering at my grandparents' house that I remember from my childhood was still going strong. My older sister was living in South Carolina, I was in Utah, a few cousins had moved on, but all my aunts, uncles, remaining cousins, and my mom still got together. I missed them so much and I wanted to be there with all my heart. There's a two hour time difference from Utah to Michigan, so while they were settling down for dinner, it was still afternoon for me. After I hung up the phone, I finally gave up and broke down. The past few nights, I had been praying to God, not for relief, but to take me away

Decisions

from this world. I was literally willing myself to die. I did not want to eat, I couldn't sleep, I was engulfed in full alcoholic dependence in order to get out of bed each day, and I gave up. The next few hours were spent crying, walking around the house remembering all the memories of Candi and the kids. I saw the person I was becoming and I was scared that I would cause my wife and kids to live the same life I had lived as a child. The perfect storm had overtaken my life and the devil was at the helm. I realize looking back how easily he creeps in and slithers into our minds. He whispers impure thoughts, and moves us around like his personal puppets when we're not paying attention. I had given up on living, and by nightfall I felt I had to end it. I couldn't stand the thought of becoming someone I grew up hating, my ex step-dad. I was upstairs in our room on the floor crying when I went decided to go to the closet and pulled out my gun. The .9mm felt light in my hand, like it belonged there. Fear started to fade away, relief and courage was what I hoped for. I needed to be released from this heartache that consumed me and the alcohol I used to drown out my sorrows. I sought courage; courage enough to end it all, courage enough to pull the trigger and be free from this savage life. I readied myself for the inevitable. I raised my hand and put the gun in my mouth. The barrel tasted bitter and metallic. You will never get the taste of steel or gun powder out of your mouth once you've taste it. To this day, when I fire a weapon, the smell and taste in the air is a gut wrenching reminder of that night. I was trembling, not knowing if I could go through with it. I was crying harder, hoping and weeping, sobbing at the notion that this was how I was going to leave this world. As I started to apply pressure and squeeze the trigger, at the perfect moment, at just the right time, at God's perfect opportunity, my phone started ringing. I lowered the weapon and thought, "NOW?!" Of all the times my phone would ring, *now* is the time? Who could it possibly be? It was my dad. We hadn't talked in a very long time. At that point, most of my family only received holiday phone calls from me. I was speechless that at that moment, when I was at my weakest, God's redemption found me in my wreckage, and of all people, used my father to do it.

God's timing is never wrong. God's timing is always perfect. God found me in the darkness and carried me out. I can look back in time and pinpoint every single moment God's grace touched my life. I look back at my decisions, my transgressions, my weaknesses, my temptations, and identify each and every time the hand of God was pressed upon me. When my dad called, I didn't pick up the phone right away. I was still in amazement that he had called at that exact moment. I took a deep breath to gain composure and I called him back. He answered and asked how I was. I told him I wasn't doing well at all and that Candi and I will be divorcing. I mustered up all the strength within me to make it through this phone call without completely breaking down again. He gave me some advice and told me I would make it through, and just breathe. He told me everything would work itself out and said there are certain people in the military I could talk to about my situation. For the first time in months, I felt a glimmer of hope. I was feeling better but still unsure of the future. I had more fear now than I ever did, because from this point forward, I had to take control of my life, clawing and scratching to make it out of the depths of the hell that I had created. I told my dad I loved him and appreciated him talking to me, having never told him what he had just saved me from.

Decisions

Sometimes the bad things that happen in our lives put us directly on the path to the best things that will ever happen to us. Everything that has ever happened in your life is preparing you for a moment that is yet to come. You may not understand today or tomorrow, but eventually, God will reveal why you went through everything you did.

"Everything you're going through is preparing you for where you're going to."
— Billy Cox, Expert Keynote Speaker/Author/Sales Trainer/Social Media Strategist -

"Hardships often prepare ordinary people for an extraordinary destiny."
— C.S. Lewis, British Novelist/Poet/Academic/Medievalist/Literary Critic/Essayist/Lay Theologian/Broadcaster/Lecturer/Christian Apologist —

"'For I know the plans I have for you,' declares the LORD, 'plans to prosper you and not to harm you, plans to give you hope and a future. 12 Then you will call on me and come and pray to me, and I will listen to you. 13 You will seek me and find me when you seek me with all your heart.'"
- Jeremiah 29:11-13 -

THE ROAD LESS TRAVELED... OR IS IT?

6

What's your why? What drives you? What is your passion? The meaning of life is found in the little things that happen to us daily; you can find meaning even in the suffering and sorrow. The ENTIRE world has one thing in common: the struggle they had to endure before they became a success. You should expect and welcome ANY adversity in your journey, because it strengthens you to be able to handle more than you thought you could. When you step out of your comfort zone, you might discover abilities and hidden talents that will surprise you. Success doesn't happen overnight. It takes a lot of work over and over again reinforcing those skills time and again. Greatness is a lot of small things done well, day after day. The same boiling water that softens the potato hardens the egg. It's about what you're made of, not the circumstances. At any given moment you have the power to say, "This is NOT how my story is going to end."

I always counted everyone else's blessings. I don't know if it was jealousy or if it was because I didn't feel anything worthwhile was happening in my life. When you count other people's blessings, you miss your own blessings happening around you. My whole life I wanted to do great big things. I felt like I was destined for greatness, but never felt like I achieved it. I knew growing up that I never wanted to waste my life away, but that's exactly what I was doing by drinking and not living my core values. I've been told that because I'm in the military that is my greatness. Only 1% of the US population joins the military, so you're the best of the best for doing so. I didn't look at it like that. I joined because of 9/11 and everyone was extremely patriotic at that time, so it seemed like something I should do. Some say I joined the military because of my father, or because both of my grandfathers fought in the Korean War. Throughout high school I had already been contemplating joining the Air Force, but I didn't know exactly when I would leave, until 2001. I had my why and I was focused on joining and making a difference.

After nearly taking my life, and after getting help for my issues, I was feeling more positive. It was a new year, a new beginning, and a new opportunity. The unit I was assigned to was due to close and we were told to put in for orders anywhere we could. I had always wanted to be a Military Training Instructor, or MTI. Most people call it a drill instructor, but it's all the same. An opportunity was there, but based on my past history, I wasn't sure I was even qualified. I applied to the position and routed all the paperwork. I was humbled at the fact that my Chief and Commander both wrote me Letters of Recommendation. They knew what I went through and told me I had an amazing testimony that can empower others to succeed. I was only seven years in to my career, almost eight, when I encountered the storms of life. I wasn't sure how much everyone knew, but I was still humbled that they would take the time to do this for me. I submitted all the required documents and within a month, I was accepted as an MTI! I was so excited, I couldn't believe it! I of all people was accepted to a high profile position, and was given the chance to influence the young men and women entering Air Force Basic Training. My co-workers had told me that what I dealt with would make me a great asset. I was incredibly anxious to find out.

A few weeks before Candi and I were to be divorced, I contacted her to tell her I had orders and I was moving. We still couldn't be around each other until the order of protection was removed. I went to court and lifted the order. We met up and talked about the whole experience and that I wanted her and the kids to move with me to Texas. At first, she wanted nothing to do with me. She already had it in her mind that a divorce was the best course of action. I remember sitting in her car at a Denny's Restaurant just bawling, telling her how much I missed her and that I was getting help. We talked about everything we had held in while we were married and laid all the issues out. I apologized for being such a horrible, inconsiderate, poor excuse of a husband. A few hours later, there was hope. After a couple weeks of slowly reintegrating back into each other's lives, it was time for the court appearance for divorce. We decided not to follow through, and our divorce decree was dismissed.

Candi and the kids moved back into the house while I went to Military Training Instructor School in San Antonio, Texas to learn how to become a drill instructor. For seven weeks, I was gone at school, while Candi stayed behind in Utah to finalize movers and ready the house to leave. Candi actually started counseling for her while I was gone to help cope with issues she was dealing with and to be a better person. We would talk on the phone, but she was still thinking, "Did our relationship really change?" I was hoping that it would, I didn't want to fight and argue with her forever. At the end of my training, our class graduated and I became a student instructor. Candi and the kids drove all the way from Utah to come watch me graduate. I was so happy to see them and couldn't believe she drove all that way with two young children. After how badly I treated her, she still unselfishly drove twenty hours to see me graduate and further my career in the Air Force. She truly does love me, and I took her for granted. I didn't deserve to have her in my life. We packed up the family and moved to San Antonio, Texas.

I was a Military Training Instructor at Lackland AFB, San Antonio, Texas, from 2009 to 2013. During those four years, the roller coaster of emotions was almost too much to bear. In the first few months, you attend a seven week school learning how to teach classes, present the material in a way that doesn't bore your audience, and to be strict but fair. We learned how to march all over again, teach drill movements, how to set up a dorm, and even how to properly use our "command voice" to call cadence and to yell at the trainees when necessary. For those seven weeks, it is half in the classroom, half on the drill pad and in the training squadrons with actual trainees. Trainees are grouped into anywhere from 40-60 person groups, called flights. The course is intense. The major downside was as a student we received zero respect from the other instructors. There was no, "Hey, how you doing, let me help, if you need anything…" It was us getting screamed at for not knowing something, screamed at for messing something up, or being told to get out of the way since we "suck" so bad. Being a student was like going back to basic training all over again because that's how we were treated. I used to drive home all the time thinking how much I hated it, I made a huge mistake, screw these guys, and they didn't even care about me. There were times I thought I should just drive my truck right into the wall because I felt like I couldn't deal with the verbal maltreatment or abuse any longer, but I didn't give up. I returned day after day, determined not to piss off everyone I knew and to be better than I was yesterday.

At the end of the seven weeks of school, and the additional eight weeks of leading my student flight through training alongside my trainer, I was awarded my instructor badge and finally earned my campaign hat. It was such a rewarding experience. This time I was greeted with smiles, handshakes, and respect. I was told by my trainer that I was treated this way to harden my skin, to put me through hell to ensure I was not a quitter, and to feel the pressures of the importance of the job I will have for the next four years. I now understood the process and why we were treated with such anger and disrespect. The pain I felt was just a part of the process. I am in charge of people's lives and it's my responsibility to prepare men and women for military service. This isn't a game or just another job. It's intense and requires hard work and dedication to excellence. I am glad I did not give up and I was ready to get started.

After student status has ended, you become a rookie instructor. You still get made fun of if you do little things wrong, but someone is there to help you through it. As long as there are no major issues, you generally don't get screamed at, which was great, because that's all I heard while I was at work. The instructors were always screaming at trainees, and I was glad I wasn't the one being screamed at anymore. We are on a timeline where these trainees need to be prepared to leave Basic Military Training and be productive in tech training, and onto their first duty station. The trainee's dates are set and any problems in training creates blockages in the pipeline and it starts with us. I would wake up at 0300, get to work at 0400, roll call 0430, wakeup 0445, fallout of the dorms for PT at 0455, PT starts at 0505, and first chow starts at 0600. The entire day is scheduled and any delays then back up everyone else. That's when our section supervisor would be yelling at us to get our flights moving. Depending on the week of training that our trainees were in, I would normally leave work around 7:30 P.M, sometimes 8pm. That's a very long day, every day. I did this for two years straight living off two big cans of Monster Energy Drinks every day. I would fall asleep in traffic, fall asleep getting a haircut, if I sat down I was going to fall asleep. However, I wouldn't take it back for anything. I have Obsessive Compulsive Disorder (OCD) and I'm super hyperactive so being an MTI was a perfect fit for me. I was left alone to lead my flight through basic training, I was able to be myself to motivate and teach my own way, using my style, and I was highly effective. At one point I even had a student, which was great because I fell in love with teaching, presenting, and inspiring the uninspired. I was trained on how to be a Student MTI Trainer, and I received two students to get fully trained. It was definitely tougher than I thought. Not only are you worried about what your flight is doing, you need to also be concerned about what the student is doing as well. You're watching him or her teach, then watching for the trainees' reactions and you need to know the right moment to step in and help, or let it be and see where it goes. By the end of the two year mark, I had lead ten flights, men and women, and all but one flight received some sort of honors award every time. With that goal accomplished, it was time to move on.

Decisions

There was an opening at what we called "Warrior Week." The trainees, towards the end of their training, would go to warrior week, or The BEAST. BEAST stands for Basic Expeditionary Airman Skills Training. Here they are taught combat survival skills, they qualify on the M-16 at the range, learn Self Aid and Buddy Care techniques, and other combat related skills. I spent the next two years as part of the Cadre Team at the BEAST site, and met some extraordinary instructors. I had a blast training trainees in these skills, and was a lot of fun. The schedule was more laid back and we had more freedom to really take the time to ensure the trainees grasped the information presented. I really came into my own and developed a solid teaching style and refined my teaching skills. God was once again working in my life. He was transforming me into the speaker I am today. I learned the most important lesson in all of this: God must break us in order to remake us. I went through my adversity and hardships, came out of it, and learned to be an excellent instructor and a presenter.

This period of my life wasn't all sunshine and rainbows. Candi and I were learning to be better partners, but we were still arguing. We thought new scenery, new people, new life; should be great. Instead we still argued, not as much, but we still pissed each other off and said hurtful things to each other. When I was on the streets leading flights, I was gone all day long, and when I got home all I wanted to do was sleep. I can only imagine how lonely Candi felt. The job was demanding and I didn't have a whole lot of time to sit and talk. We would text, or she would stop by during lunch so we could at least see each other for a few minutes, but for the most part, I was gone all day long. I also barely got to see my kids. We were in a new place and didn't know very many people, and she was taking care of the kids all by herself. As I grew as an

Decisions

instructor, I knew when I was most needed at work and when I could leave early. I started accomplishing more during the week so I wasn't at work all weekend. With the new position at The BEAST, I didn't work weekends anymore. I now had more of an opportunity to spend time with my family and pursue other ventures.

Candi and I still were not where we needed to be, but we were making it. We had split up again during my transition from pushing flights to moving over to The BEAST. I stayed with a friend for a little while, just to give her some space. We had grown apart from the long hours and stressful nature of yelling all day. We weren't fighting as bad, but we had also let people into our lives that played both sides and didn't have our best interests at heart. We would talk every once in a while, but I think it was more to see how the kids were doing and if they needed anything. I missed my family and after a couple months, I was able to come home. We talked everything out again, even decided to go to marriage counseling. I was extremely against it before this, but I figured what do I have to lose? Our neighbor even tried to help us. She gave us a Kirk Cameron movie, called "Fireproof." It was a movie about fireproofing your marriage and following this teaching for forty days. I printed out the journal and I got to work. During the forty days, I felt a transformation. I wasn't so mad about the little things anymore. There's a saying that says, "Don't sweat the small stuff." My problem was I wanted to fight every battle and never knew how to pick and choose which battle was worth fighting. Pretty soon, I was fighting everything and everyone, and it drove me crazy. I had to learn to get out of my own way so that I could see the way, so that there could be a way. At the end of my forty day journey, I felt more relaxed and I had more love for my wife than I did

Decisions

before. Plus, marriage counseling helped, too. I was communicating better, and displaying it better, too. I had a problem expressing my emotions from all the hurt in my past. I thought if I gave my whole heart and put myself out there, my heart would get destroyed again. Candi stuck by me through all of my hurt, pain, and crazy behavior. I don't know anyone else that would have done the same. I was back home with my family and it felt great.

I had weekends off now. What do I do with my spare time? I went to storage auctions and bought storage units that had gone unpaid. We found some amazing items, and I use that term loosely. We found silver, jewelry, DVDs, furniture, but we have also found some not so nice items such as leather chaps and a strap-on adult toy. You think I'm joking? This was the worst unit ever! There was always that one unit that made you question why you did what you did. I was finding everything from 1940s cameras, 96 piece china sets, gaming systems, but I bought that one unit that scared me. There were packages of condoms, dirty magazines and pictures, plus the not so nice items I mentioned earlier. This was a complete trash haul off. That's the risk you take in this business. Candi and I eventually acquired so many items that we decided to open a store, and Vintage Dreams was born. We were making a few hundred dollars selling at a garage sale at our house, but we needed to sell more volume. We had a ton of inventory and were so excited at how this all developed. We opened up our store in a plaza mixed with storefronts and restaurants. We did fairly well, but not as well as I thought we would. We were making the same amount of money as we were at a garage sale and I couldn't figure out why. Instead of closing or giving up, every month or so, we would rearrange the store while adding in a few more items. We also sold online so we were pulling in a decent amount of money, but nothing like on the Storage Wars TV Show. I would have loved to find something worth a few thousand, but we never did. I was loving this adventure, buying other people's items, and digging through their stuff like a treasure hunter. At one point, we started saving up all the loose change and by the end of the year we saved enough to buy Christmas presents on that change alone. We were happy and I didn't want it to end.

Don't get me wrong, running a store is hard. You are forced to deal with all types of people and it really tests your patience. We asked one of our close friends to partner with us to make this store even bigger. We expanded and grew our client base stronger. I loved it when our regulars would come in and chat with us to see what we found in our units. I was amazed how interested people were about items we would bring in. My most favorite items we had was a collection of lunchboxes. We had *He-Man, Care Bears, Dukes of Hazard, Transformers*, and numerous others from the 80s and 90s. I loved finding items from my childhood. We generated a lot of interest because we would seek out items for people who wanted to relive memories from their childhood. I sold a gas pump phone to a guy in Houston, Texas who was absolutely thrilled to have it. A 12 year old girl was ecstatic when I sold her a 1940s Kodak camera for twenty dollars. It was then that I was sure what my purpose was.

I wanted to make people happy, somehow. Not like a clown, a comedian, or a magician, but someone who makes dreams come true. I have always wanted to make a positive impactful difference in people's lives, I just didn't know how. Then it dawned on me; I was already making an impact serving as an MTI. I was the first person the trainees saw when they entered basic training. I was the

Decisions

first impression they received, and they would formulate opinions about the Air Force based on their interactions with the instructors. I made it a point now to be intentional about the difference I was making, even more than I was when I was on the street leading flights. At The BEAST, we received new flights every week. I wanted to leave a lasting impression the trainees could take with them. This process birthed my passion for motivation and resilience. I would motivate the trainees every second I could. I would watch other motivational speakers such as Eric Thomas, Les Brown, Billy Cox, Zig Ziglar, and many others. I listened, learned, and researched how to motivate people, and how to deliver the message. I was already an instructor. I presented material all day every day. I was being intentional about refining my skills, looking for more ways to be a better presenter and speaker. I fell in love with being in front of people, seeing the difference I was making, and seeing the looks on their faces when they nodded in approval of what it was I was delivering. My boss and a few of my co-workers would call me the "Master Motivator" because I was always getting everyone fired up and excited about something. It felt great to pour into people's lives and help them through whatever it was they were dealing with. I had found my true calling. I knew what my purpose was; to be a motivational speaker, life coach, to inspire the uninspired, and to light a fire in those who felt they had no purpose.

I felt like I was destined for greatness. I had this fire burning inside me. I wanted to do some amazing things and change people's lives, but I didn't know how. If I won the lottery, I would donate the money. If I could save someone's life, I wanted to do it. I felt like I needed to do something huge, like invent the light bulb, or the cell phone. I had a passion in me that needed to get out and change the community in some way, but I didn't know how. I would always hear from those closest to me that I was accomplishing just that by preparing men and women for military duty. It didn't feel that way though. There has to be more to life than this, there has to be more to it than I was experiencing. I was struggling to find an outlet or a method to get out there and change lives. I found out later that if God can trust you in the small things, He will bless you with the big things. I believe He was still working within me that whole time. He was stirring up my spirit, but at the time, I didn't give Him the credit. I was still unsure about religion and had a lot of questions. Everyone around me seemed so sure, I felt like I was the only one questioning my faith. I was raised Roman Catholic, but when I turned 18, I walked away from God. It was never personal. I was forced to go to church, communion, confession, confirmation; it was my family's decision for me. I would've rather slept in than go to church, but I was forced to go. From the time I was thirteen until I turned eighteen I was part of a youth group called the Squires. The Knights of Columbus is a Catholic fraternal organization for men, and the boys become Squires to learn about serving as Knights. My grandfather on my mom's side introduced me to it. I loved it, kept me out of trouble, and taught me about the Catholic faith, but when I was old enough, I turned my back on God.

I was amazed at how someone can be so strong in their faith, yet go through so much adversity. I always thought since I was a believer that I would be saved from hardships, but it's just the opposite. As soon as my life got hard, I would curse God and ask where He was. I didn't feel close to Him, I didn't feel like He was working for me, and I felt betrayed. I prayed to stop drinking, I prayed that the hot chow hall chick and I would be together forever, I prayed as best I could, but nothing happened. By age 23, I had stopped talking to God. I didn't need Him, I didn't want Him, and it just felt useless. Growing up, I didn't have a relationship with Jesus. I was told what to believe and taught what was in the Bible. It wasn't personal for me, it felt forced and something I wasn't interested in. When our neighbor gave us the Fireproof movie, I was thinking, "Oh really, a God movie? I don't need that." In the movie, Kirk Cameron said the same thing. It got me thinking though. What if it was what I needed? Maybe I did need Jesus in my life. Our neighbor was always praying over us, some of our friends would invite us to church, but I never wanted any of it. Candi and the kids started attending a church with her friend, but I stayed home. I was still so bitter that God would allow all the terrible moments of my life to occur and I wanted nothing from Him. Candi would plead with me to go to church with her and I told her if I was to ever find a church worth going to, then I would go, but since it's not worth it, I'm never going. Sometimes, our words come back to bite us.

In 2012, Lackland AFB was rocked by a sexual assault scandal. Approximately 36 MTIs were charged with various counts of rape, sexual assault, sexual misconduct, and maltreatment. I could not believe some of my closest friends were assaulting female trainees. We were supposed to be the example, the standard trainees should live up to, and the most professional group in the Air Force. Instead, we were labeled sexual predators, deviants, and our instructor core was tainted. It wasn't just a select group. There were instructors all over the base being accused of maltreatment, various degrees of abuse, inappropriate relationships, and misconduct. No one was safe. The scandal overshadowed every positive moment the instructors had accomplished, and tarnished

Decisions

the instructor core as a whole. A lot of changes came down after this. A lot of instructors were disgusted at the actions of those who misused their authority. I was fed up and ready to move on, as was everyone else.

At the end of 2012, I got my wish, just not exactly how I planned. I was working with a group of trainees when some cadre came over and was gathering trainees for a meeting. This particular week, we had received some of the worst trainees we had ever dealt with. They were lazy, didn't care, were not following our directions, and we had to scream at them most of the week. Our team had gathered the trainees together to talk to them about their behavior. There were still those who were not listening, talking while we were talking, and we said enough. We identified a handful of trainees who we thought were disruptive, and as punishment, they were to police the area for trash and pull up any weeds that were growing around the tents. One trainee stepped forward in defiance. He said that he was not going to pull weeds and that the punishment was crap. He said that he was not there to pull weeds, but to learn, since he was an Airman and not getting paid to pull weeds. I lost it. I screamed at him like he had just kicked my dog. I locked him up at attention and threw out every disparaging remark I could to let him know how much of a piece of crap he was, and if he did not follow my orders, I would call Security Forces and have him thrown in jail. I then turned my rage on the rest of our flight and told them how much they sucked and how I couldn't wait until they left. I thought it was typical drill instructor behavior, but there were a few who thought I overreacted. The trainees were dismissed to carry out their punishment.

As I calmed down, I remember feeling deflated. What was basic training coming to? I had been there almost four years and I NEVER had a trainee talk back or defy orders. I had a conversation with my section supervisor about the situation and he said he'd handle it. He went to our site and yelled at the defiant trainee, while trying to inspire him to do better. We walked away thinking this would be the last time we would have to deal with insubordination. We were wrong. The trainees left two days later, and that's when I got the phone call. When the trainees returned to their dorms, the defiant individual filed a critique against me for verbal maltreatment. I could not believe that someone who defied our orders, who was disruptive and disrespectful, dropped a critique accusing me of maltreatment and said I was acting unprofessional. I was disgusted. An investigation was launched and the findings supported his claims of my maltreatment. I was removed from training immediately, interrogated about the sequence of events, and assigned to our warehouse away from trainees. The investigation process concluded two weeks later and I was administered a Letter of Reprimand. This meant I was permanently removed as an MTI, and no longer allowed to be an instructor. One month shy of completing four years I was removed from training and my Commendation Medal was withheld. After four long years, and everything I went through, I was ostracized and thrown away like trash. The investigation revealed that I had sworn in front of trainees, which was deemed unprofessional. The Commander wrote a policy stating that swearing, or using profanity, was unacceptable and would not be tolerated. At first, my leadership wanted to court martial me for violating a Commander's written policy, but ultimately was talked down by my immediate supervisors. I received my reprimand, bad marks on my performance report, and given an

Decisions

assignment to Seymour Johnson AFB, North Carolina. This was one of the most humiliating moments of my life.

Candi and I had built an amazing life in Texas. We had wonderful friends, a stable support system, and it was so hard to move. Although we were both ready to leave the instructor life behind, leaving our close friends was extremely hard. We decided at one point we had to retire in Texas. We loved the area where we lived, and the people we grew close to made the assignment an amazing experience. Leaving was very hard, but we packed up and headed east. Prior to leaving Texas, I filed an application with Seymour Johnson's housing office to move into base housing. We were accepted, and we had a four bedroom house waiting for us when we arrived. As a family we LOVE road trips. Every chance we get, we take a road trip somewhere. We drove eighteen hours east to visit with my older sister and brother-in-law in South Carolina. It was so nice to relax and try to unwind from the fast paced instructor life. We spent the weekend recuperating with family, but then it was time to leave.

We arrived at Seymour Johnson AFB, North Carolina. I was excited to return to my career field and begin working on aircraft again. I was rejuvenated with new people, new scenery, and new opportunities. I even met airman I once taught in basic training, which was exciting because you never really know what happens to them after training. You just always hope that you did a good enough job that they become productive members of the military, and not kicked out for being stupid. I was introduced to my new unit, but what I received was not what I had anticipated. No one was interested in me or who I was; they wanted to hear stories about the Lackland sex scandal. Everyone wanted to hear about how I used to yell at people, how I acted as an MTI, and wanted to hear

Decisions

stories about the craziness I witnessed from trainees. I wanted to focus more on becoming proficient as a Crew Chief since I had not worked on aircraft in four years. Sometimes, we just have to go with the flow, and if that meant my acceptance into the unit came with story time, well then that's what I was going to do. I spent six months working side by side with some of the best maintainers I had ever worked with. These guys were smart, energetic, and worked very well together. The moral in the unit was super high, and squadron pride was at the forefront. I was blessed to be in a unit that took care of their people, ensured they were setup for success, and that they came to work with a positive attitude.

I would love to go on and talk about how this lasted forever, but nothing ever does. When one door closes, another will open. We can choose to walk through the door or be shoved through the threshold. Either way, the decision will be made, either by us or for us. Whenever you find yourself doubting how far you can go, remember how far you have come. Remember everything you have faced, all the battles you have won, and the fears you overcame. Faith is not the absence of doubt. Faith is the overcoming of doubt. What would happen next would alter the course of my life, forever.

Decisions

"He who has a WHY can endure any HOW."
– Friedrich Nietzsche, German Philosopher/Cultural
Critic/Poet/Latin and Greek Scholar –

"Strength doesn't come from what you can do. It comes
from overcoming the things you once thought you
couldn't."
– Rikki Rogers, Writer/Marketer/Graphic Designer –

"I can do all things through Christ who strengthens me."
- Philippians 4:13

THE WILL, THE DECISION, THE TRANSFORMATION

7

The ability to correct my mistakes is the most important lesson I learned in everything I've endured so far. Endured.....what does that mean? The dictionary tell us it means to withstand, to tolerate, to suffer. Almost everything I "endured" was my own fault. Every decision made affects the very next decision. I wrecked cars, I wrecked relationships, I wrecked friendships, and I left wreckage everywhere I went, but, God finds redemption in our lives, even in the wreckage. There is no one more forgiving than Jesus Christ and I am so thankful for His salvation. I walked away from religion, I didn't agree with a lot of what was said in church or displayed in public. I had a lot of questions and very little faith that God is who He said He is. We tend to believe ideas that are tangible. If I can see it then it is real, if I can smell or taste it, then I'll acknowledge its existence. Life is not that cut and dry. Events happen that we can't explain, unexpected blessings come into our lives when we least expect it.

In 2013, I found out that I was due to be promoted. I was incredibly excited to be progressing in my career, especially at a new duty station. With a new promotion came new responsibility. I was asked if I wanted an opportunity to deploy with another unit to gain experience at a new position I was applying for. After discussing the opportunity with Candi, I decided to accept the offer. I went to work for another unit to integrate with their personnel prior to the deployment. I was hoping for a smooth transition but I was met with disappointment and resentment.

I was introduced to my new boss and I will never forget what he said. I went to shake his hand and let him know that I was his new Expediter. As an Expediter, my job is to control the flow of maintenance on the flightline and ensure everyone is performing at peak performance. I'm in charge of directing maintenance and ensure that the aircraft are getting fixed quickly, maintenance personnel have all the tools and equipment required for the task, and everyone is safe. As soon as the boss saw me he said, "You're not expediter material." He didn't even know me. He passed judgement on me before I could even explain who I was, what I've done, where I've been, and how excited I was for this opportunity. I had a feeling I would be working for a terrible leader.

Before I left, we found out we were pregnant. Completely unexpected, not planned, and we were scared since I was deploying to the Middle East. I felt guilty for leaving her and worried what would happen after I left. I had spent a lot of time on the road during our marriage, but not seven months at a time. This deployment would be the longest we would spend away from each other. Even when we were split up before, it wasn't for this long.

Our unit deployed and we were off to a terrible start. The first day, one of the guys lost his headset. Soon after, some equipment was damaged and our leadership was irate. The personnel I was in charge of were losing motivation fast and I knew I needed to pump them up. I started letting a few people off work early as an incentive to work hard. There were still those who chose to work slow, talk rather than work, and do as little as possible. I yelled at them and told them we are deployed in support of missions to protect our country and our allies, and that this mission is a big deal. When you're away from your family, in a face paced, high profile scenario, it's easy to lose focus. After two months, a few mishaps, and constant frustration, I and a few others were fired from our positions. I couldn't believe I volunteered to deploy to the Middle East and was fired. I was asked what I wanted to do instead of expediting, and I told them I wanted to go home since my wife was pregnant. If I'm not here doing the job I came here to do, then send me home. My leadership told me I was not going home, I was switching shifts, and I was back working alongside everyone else as a Crew Chief. I was furious, sad, unmotivated, and I didn't care about anyone anymore. I didn't exactly give up on my team, but my faith in that leadership was nonexistent.

We had a few friends who helped out while I was gone, but, the support system my unit had in place was utterly broken and useless. Candi fell down the stairs in her third month of pregnancy due to a sudden onset of vertigo. She was walking up the stairs to bed when, halfway up, became dizzy and tumbled down the steps. She stopped herself a half way down and struggled to regain her composure. She called her support system but no one was available to help. Allegedly, everyone was busy and unable to come to her aid. Luckily, one of our good friends, who was also pregnant, came to her rescue. To this day, it sickens me to think how close we were to losing our baby because someone was too selfish to come

Decisions

and help us. Candi fell down the stairs twice while I was deployed due to having vertigo, and the key support system that was supposed to be in place never came to her rescue.

While I was deployed, Candi found The Bridge Church. That same friend who was pregnant and came to her aid, was the same one who went to that church. The Bridge has a military ministry called "Call To Arms", for active duty military and veterans to connect with each other. She would tell me how amazing it felt to be amongst those who were also dealing with issues and didn't judge. I was still skeptical because I didn't feel like I needed religion to solve my problems. She had found a support system within the church, which was great for her, but it was not for me. She would tell me all about The Bridge Church during my almost yearlong deployment. I was very happy for her that she was smiling and doing well while I was gone. She kept trying to sell me on why I needed to attend this church, just for me to check it out and see for myself. Religion wasn't for me, I didn't feel a connection to it like other people did. I didn't need to believe in something I couldn't see and blame it on something I had no proof even existed. I told her to keep going to church, but to count me out.

We had grown closer to each other while I was away. We had no choice but to finally iron out some of the problems in our relationship. We would video chat sometimes, but even then, we were still forced to talk about things you would not normally talk about. We still after six years of marriage had unresolved issues, so we worked through some of those issues and it seriously felt as if a weight of stress was lifted. I was so worried about making it home in time for Makenzie's birth, but Candi was so amazing at keeping me updated and scheduling a

Decisions

phone call for me while she was at the doctor's appointments. She was so strong with handling the pregnancy alone, being both parents to our two kids, and keeping up with housework and paying bills. I couldn't have asked her to do any more, she was so strong.

After seven months of living in a tent in the desert, I made it home in time to see Makenzie born. She was born 4/14/2014 at 1400, five days past her due date. It was amazing! I remember telling the doctor to put her back in because it was 1357, to just wait like three minutes and her birthday and time will be all fourteens. Candi said, "Oh, NO! She's been in long enough, time for her to go." Makenzie was so beautiful! It took everything I had not to cry. I was so happy, proud, excited, anxious, and so many other feelings I couldn't begin to describe. I could hardly wait for this moment. I was always gone when the other kids were little, and Candi already had Gaven before we met. I finally had a child of my own that I witnessed being born and I could come home to every night. I was truly blessed.

Not long after Makenzie was born, I returned to work. The deployment was a complete disaster, and the remaining leadership was disbanded and sent to other duty sections. Luckily, one of them hired me for a new position that was opening up. With everything that went on during the deployment, it was nice to be given another chance and set up for success this time around. I accepted the position and was beyond ready to start a new chapter. It's amazing how we can look back and pinpoint exactly all the blessings that God gives to us. Had I not deployed with that unit and met the supervision I had, or endured what I did, I may not have been considered for this position. God's timing is truly perfect. When we don't see a way I know God has already made a way.

Decisions

A few months after Makenzie was born, I was settling into my new job. I was enjoying life and our new family. Well, you know that means, as soon as you get comfortable, all hell breaks loose. I received a yearlong remote tour assignment to Korea. Remote tours are where your family is not allowed to accompany you and you must go by yourself. I was due to leave at the beginning of 2015, ten months after my initial notification. I was bummed. I was devastated that I had to leave right before Makenzie's first birthday. I told Candi that since she's going to church, she had better pray for my orders to be canceled. She kept telling me how I needed to go with her and pray myself. I kept refusing, until one day, I couldn't take it anymore and I attended a service kicking and screaming.

I attended a service with full skepticism and closed mindedness. I was thinking this is going to be boring, the preacher just tells you what you want to hear, just wants you to give the church money, etc. The first service I attend at The Bridge and what do they talk about in the sermon? The pastor is preaching about how everyone needs to serve God by giving their tithe. I turned and Candi and gasped, "SEE! The church only wants money! I told you that I was right. I'm leaving. I'll be in the car." Candi pleaded with me to stay and hear the Pastor out. I sat through the sermon, arms crossed, mad the rest of the time. After service, Candi begged me to keep going back and that it was going to be different each time. I was so closed off at this point, I didn't care what she said as long as she left me alone. I was pleasantly surprised a few Sundays later when the Pastor preached on different subjects and felt like they were relevant. As I continued attending service, I felt more and more open to the

Decisions

Pastor's message. Pretty soon, I would wake up excited to go to church.

Our church has a slogan I absolutely love that says, "Belong Before You Believe." I firmly believe that is key. I didn't believe in anything religious, but I did feel relaxed and not judged when I came to this church. Everyone is so kind, standing in line for their coffee, wearing everything from dress clothes to shorts and sandals. I have never once felt judged nor have I witnessed someone judging another person. Plus, our church is one pyro technic away from a Bon Jovi concert. Our band rocks! Every Sunday when we worship, the lights go out and we are immersed in amazing songs, glorious voices singing His praise, and the music touches your soul. The more I went, the more I felt a transformation happening inside of me. God was working in my life the entire time. He was in me stirring things around, and tossing stuff out like it was spring cleaning. I didn't feel the weight of the world on my back anymore. I didn't feel the temptations to drink and be rude to my wife and kids. My self-defeating behaviors seemed to dissipate little by little, Sunday after Sunday, and I felt calmer and more at ease. A breathe of fresh air was breathed into my life, and I felt renewed and rejuvenated. Towards the end of 2014, our family never missed a Sunday service, and we started committing ourselves to Christ as a family.

There's a quote by Dave Willis, who is a pastor, author, and blogger about marriage, and he said, "Great marriages don't happen by luck or by accident. They are the result of a consistent investment of time, thoughtfulness, forgiveness, affection, prayer, mutual respect, and a rock-solid commitment between husband and wife." I believe this could be true for any relationship though. As God was pouring into our family, we were all changing as well, and we started pouring into each other. We stopped bringing electronic devices to the dinner table, turned the TV off, we prayed before each meal, and we talked to each other at dinner about our day and the blessings we had in our life. It has been a wonderful experience and transformation.

God opens doors no man can close. He will also close doors that no man can open. Out of nowhere, I was informed that my orders to Korea had been canceled. We had been praying and hoping, and truthfully there was a part of me that was skeptical but I was quickly proven wrong. When my orders were canceled, I met a man that would forever change my life. On base we have different civilians that play a major role in the day-to-day functions of an Air Force Base. One of those roles was our Community Support Coordinator. This position works alongside the base commander. I met our Community Support Coordinator at a youth event and told him how I was a prior MTI and have been an instructor for many years. His eyes lit up and suggested I become a Resilience Trainer. I didn't know what resilience was, other than how we bounce back from "stuff". He said that's exactly right and you teach other people how to do just that. I accepted his offer, attended training, and have now been a Master Resilience Trainer for a few years. I have met some amazing people with amazing testimonies. God put in me the ability to teach, train, present, motivate, and inspire by any means necessary. As a Resilience Trainer, this is just another outlet for me to tell my story and help others through their adversity. I teach skillsets in the Mental, Physical, Social, and Spiritual domains of resilience that strengthen us, and help us, through our adversity.

Resilience is the strength of our spirit to recover from adversity. It is our ability to withstand, recover, and grow in the face of stress and adversity. When we experience disappointment, loss, or tragedy, we find hope and courage to carry on. Humor lightens the load when it seems too heavy. We overcome obstacles by tapping into a deep well of faith and endurance. At times of loss, we come together for comfort. We grieve and then move on. We create new memories. We discover the learning that comes from hardships. We don't cower in the face of challenges. We engage fully in the dance of life. Resilience can be taught and strengthened. It is a reinforced behavior.

Sometimes our lives have to be completely shaken up, changed, and rearranged to relocate us to the place we're meant to be. It can take days, months, or even years for that transformation to be complete. Recognizing the process is very hard while walking through the fire, but when you get to the other side, and you compartmentalize everything you have been through and how it caused you to become stronger, it is in that moment you realize how powerful your will truly is. God is and always has been in control of our lives and I am so thankful I was welcomed back into His kingdom. Like the parable of the prodigal son, I felt God's warmth when I returned to Him in surrender and let Him direct my steps.

Today, Makenzie is two years old. Candi and I are still going strong. I love my wife so much and am so thankful and humbled she stood by me through all of my issues, treating her badly, and ruining our relationship. There's no one else I would rather spend my life with, and I am looking forward to our future together. We have been through hell and back in our relationship, and I thank God for somehow keeping us together. We still have ups and downs, but that's life. I love her so much more now than I ever have and it's because I opened myself up to the

Decisions

Lord for healing. Candi and I serve every Sunday at The Bridge Church in Princeton, North Carolina. We are Life Coaches for Life Group Leaders who hold small group bible study. We also lead our own small home group that meets Sunday evenings for fellowship and bible study. Two years ago, I was kicking and screaming all the way to church. Now, I can't imagine my life without God. I have surrendered my life to Jesus Christ, and I know, with or without my permission, God is going to move in ways to further His Kingdom. Our Pastor, Ferrell Hardison, is truly one of kind. I'm learning from him how to take my life to a HNL: "Hole 'Nother Level", by putting God first. I am also a motivational speaker and I travel around and speak at different youth camps, high schools, conferences, and associations. I have had to get out of my own way so that God can make a way in my life. Since I have done this, I have seen a change in my family and in myself. I am so thankful for God's grace and forgiveness. Just like the prodigal son in the bible, I have come home, and God the Father has welcomed me back.

I want to inspire people. I want someone to look at me and say "Because of you I did not give up."

"You, dear children, are from God and overcome them, because the One who is in you is greater than the ones who is in the world." - 1 John 4:4 -

"²⁰ So he got up and went to his father. But while he was still a long way off, his father saw him and was filled with compassion for him; he ran to his son, threw his arms around him and kissed him. ²¹ The son said to him, 'Father, I have sinned against heaven and against you. I am no longer worthy to be called your son.' ²² But the father said to his servants, 'Quick! Bring the best robe and put it on him. Put a ring on his finger and sandals on his feet. ²³ Bring the fattened calf and kill it. Let's have a feast and celebrate. ²⁴ For this son of mine was dead and is alive again; he was lost and is found.' So they began to celebrate."   – Luke 15:20-24 -

Made in the USA
Columbia, SC
13 September 2017